now instead of continuing the united meetings once a week
as proposed, they wish to meet amongst themselves for prayer
- when Mr Lennam comes to lecture on the revivals in Ireland
having been an eye witness, Mr Price will devote 3 eve.s in
the week previously for united prayer. They meet at school
room for prayer & last eve.g, Graystone alone prayed.

Fri. 27th

We all rose at 1st & breakfasted at 1/2 past, then Chs & Mr
Gilsold started for Railsworth. the Morn.g was wet
Mr Smith came in to tea & P. & I inform'd him that
we c.d now raise only £26 a year for him, he receiv.d
it very nicely & s.d that the village was greatly indebted
to our family for what we had already done & he that
we had been most generous & liberal, I gave him 4/-
to make up 3/6 for Betty Miller (church money) 2/6
for Hannah Vincent & the same for Thos. Woolley
he v.d sick till after supper. — Mr C. saw B. in bed
this morn & exam.d her, s.d to my joy that there was no
reason why she might not soon be restored, poor girl
she passes a great deal of mucous & fleshy matter, but she
evidently seems much better & hope she'll keep so.

Sat. 28th

This morn had quite a trial, to engage in family pray.
er & yet c.d not bear to neglect it because Chs is out
I earnestly sought divine help & then call'd Esther in - for
the 1st time conducted family prayer without a book
tho' I had one at hand in case I sh.d be too nervous to
proceed, & God helped me to raise the family altar
to His name, it was quite a trial to me, I've never en
-gaged aloud before anyone but Kate, in eve.g went thro'
it again. This afternoon went down to Miss This'k
see if she c.d go & collect for Dorcas society but she was
going out so I went & p.d Brown, Fletcher, met Mrs
Cornwall & had chat with her, p.d Cross & Arkell.
Have only read once this week to my old friends, I fear
Mrs Dickson is very dark, they were all glad to see me

THE SECRET DIARY OF

Sarah Thomas

1860-1865

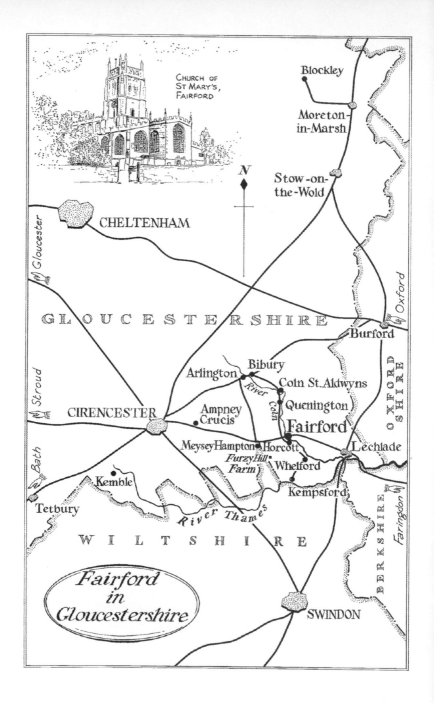

CHURCH OF
ST MARY'S,
FAIRFORD

N

Blockley

Moreton-
in-Marsh

Stow-on-
the-Wold

CHELTENHAM

Gloucester

GLOUCESTERSHIRE

Burford

Oxford

Stroud

Bibury

Arlington

River Coln

Coln St. Aldwyns

Quenington

CIRENCESTER

Ampney
Crucis

River Coln

Fairford

OXFORDSHIRE

Bath

Meysey Hampton

Horcott

Lechlade

*Furzy Hill
Farm*

Whelford

Kemble

Kempsford

BERKSHIRE

Tetbury

River Thames

Faringdon

WILTSHIRE

*Fairford
in
Gloucestershire*

SWINDON

THE SECRET DIARY OF

Sarah Thomas

1860-1865

EDITED BY JUNE LEWIS

THE WINDRUSH PRESS · GLOUCESTERSHIRE

First published in Great Britain by
The Windrush Press
Little Window, High Street,
Moreton-in-Marsh
Gloucestershire GL56 0LL

Telephone: 0608 652012
Fax: 0608 652125

British Library Cataloguing in Publication Data
A catalogue record for this book is available from
the British Library

ISBN 0 900075 38 4

Production by Greenshires Icon, Exeter, Devon

DEDICATION

For my dear friends, Colin, Lucy and David
for their unfailing interest and encouragement

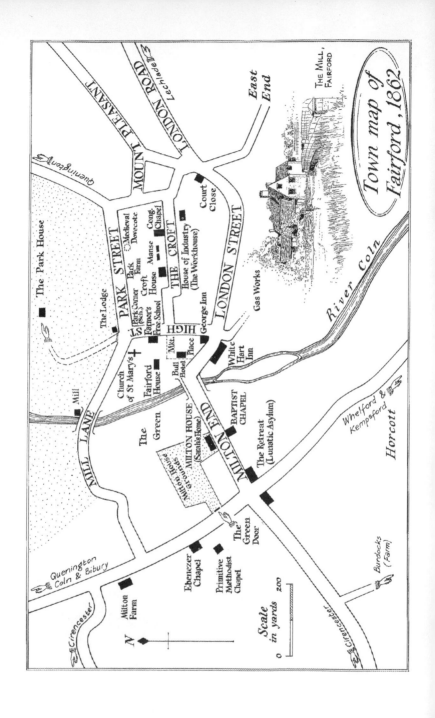

Town map of Fairford, 1862

Quenington

Coln & Bibury

Cirencester

N

Scale
in yards
0   200

Milton Farm

Ebenezer Chapel

Primitive Methodist Chapel

The Green Door

Burdocks (Farm)

Cirencester

Quenington

Mill

MILL LANE

The Park House

The Lodge

Church of St Mary's

The Fairford House

The Green

Milton House Grounds

MILTON HOUSE (Sarah's Home)

MILTON END

Bull Hotel

Mkt. Place

HIGH ST.

PARK STREET

Park Corner Farm (Sch.)

Palmer's Free School

Medieval Dovecote

Park Farm

Croft House

Manse

Cong. Chapel

THE CROFT

House of Industry (The Workhouse)

Court Close

George Inn

White Hart Inn

BAPTIST CHAPEL

The Retreat (Lunatic Asylum)

MOUNT PLEASANT

MOUNT ROAD

LONDON ROAD

Lechlade

East End

LONDON STREET

Gas Works

River Coln

THE MILL, FAIRFORD

Whelford & Kempsford

Horcott

Contents

List of Illustrations

Editor's note and acknowledgements

I first became acquainted with Sarah's diary when I was approached to assist Olwen Lloyd of Oxford with research for a thesis on which she was working on Non-Conformity. Mrs Lloyd and I met on several occasions and we both got completely engrossed in Sarah Thomas's life and family, vicariously through the diary which had been lent to her by Dr Vaisey, Keeper of Western Manuscripts at the Bodleian Library.

The task, initially, was beset by problems arising from the fact that there were two John Thomas's, both grandfathers of Sarah. I had grown up with the story of John Thomas, the first Baptist Missionary to Bengal, as he was a Fairford man – so I was delighted to find, after much unscrambling of family deeds and documents, wills and agreements, that this colourful character was indeed an ancestor of Sarah. Many names are abbreviated in the diary and this, too, exercised my local knowledge and called for research to identify various characters.

Quite by coincidence, I had a telephone call some time later, from one of my old students asking if I knew anything about the Thomas family of Fairford. Paul Dabson told me that the grandfather of a friend of his had found a small diary 'in a woodshed' and was fascinated by it, but as he was a North Country man he had no means of identifying the diarist or the people she mentioned. The entries alone were enough to hold his attention. On reading them I was completely ecstatic to discover it was the diary of 1862 – a vital link in the story. This sheer stroke of chance seemed to indicate that I was the lynch pin on which Sarah's story hinged. After considerable persuasion Dr Vaisey sold the diaries on which I had worked with Mrs Lloyd to me. He had bought them initially from an antiquarian bookseller in Hampshire many years previously with the intention of publishing them himself, as he also recognised therein lay an interesting story of an interesting family. I have now lived with and worked on Sarah's diaries many more years than it took her to write them – I only hope I have done justice to her, and her secrets.

I would like to thank the following for their help and co-operation: Mrs Olwen Lloyd for first introducing me to Sarah's diaries and her painstaking research on many aspects of Non-Conformity records; Dr Vaisey, Keeper of Western Manuscripts, Bodleian Library, Oxford; Paul Dabson for obtaining for me the missing link in the diaries; the many records offices who have allowed me facilities for research, in particular the Records Office staff of Gloucester, and the staff of various Libraries and Press Libraries; the Archivist of the National Library of Jamaica; Brindley Sangster and Uty Smith of Jamaica; John Drinkwater, Editor of *Cotswold Life*, in which an abridged series of diary entries were published; the members of the United Church (the old Baptist Chapel), Fairford who so ably performed my dramatised version of the story of Sarah to commemorate the tenth anniversary of the United Church. I am also grateful to Lord Bathurst for his interest and help on The Woodhouse; Mr and Mrs P J Foot of Meysey Hampton, and Nan Brinn for allowing me to sketch parts of her house. Finally, but by no means least of all, my thanks to Victoria Huxley, my publisher, for her enthusiasm and patience in getting Sarah's story in print.

Introduction

The diaries, spanning the years 1860-65, are those of Sarah Thomas, the daughter of a Baptist Minister, who lived in the ancient Cotswold market town of Fairford in Gloucestershire. At the time of writing her diaries, Sarah was thirty-seven years of age, unmarried, and had lost both parents leaving her head of the household of Milton House, a substantial family home which stood opposite the Baptist Chapel in Milton Street. Two older brothers, William Newitt Thomas and John Anderson Thomas, had emigrated to Australia. Charles Kingsley, a half-brother through her mother's former marriage, lived for a great deal of his time at Milton House with Sarah and her younger sister, Kate, although he had his own property at Furzy Hill and farmed land at Burdocks near by; in the 1851 Census he is recorded as an accountant. Kate, often referred to as Kitty in Sarah's diaries, suffered from bad health and was a constant cause of concern to Sarah.

The diaries are highly personal; unlike the journals of many Victorian ladies which have found their way into print, Sarah's entries, as will be seen by the reader, were written as secret confidences, often almost as confessionals when she questions her motives or examines her feelings. They were never meant for anyone else's eyes for they are not merely the domestic daily happenings of family life, they are frank and revealing and intimate. And herein lay their value and charm for they tell a love story with dignified drama of strong passion restrained by convention and pious prejudices. Jane Austen might have written the story in an earlier age. In fact, there are many small glimpses of an almost Austen-type sharpness in Sarah's thumbnail sketches of some of the characters that people her life. But these are the diarist's own personal observations and style as she does not appear to have any pretensions to writing, or modelling her thoughts on any popular author. On the contrary, she makes a point in one entry of confessing to reading a novel when she thought her time should have been more gainfully employed to strengthen her spiritual command and comprehension.

Through such intimate revelations emerges Sarah herself, no longer young but with a youthful spirit bordering on the rebellious, a characteristic to which she readily admits. She no doubt inherited this from her maternal grandfather, John Thomas – a really interesting scallywag in his chequered career as ship's surgeon. Said to be the despair of his Deacon father, John Thomas threw himself into pious penance whenever excessive drinking and ruinous gambling brought him to death's door or debtors' prison. He eventually became one of the 'great men of Gloucestershire', finding his talents channelled eventually in the missionary cause to become the first Baptist mission doctor to Bengal. Sarah, also, has an almost ambivalent attitude to religion. She obviously found it difficult at times to live up to the strict doctrine of her upbringing, resorting to scolding her maids and praying passionately with equal energy, particularly when her love life did not run smoothly, which it rarely did! She copied out great chunks of scriptural texts and exhorted herself to piety, yet there are glimpses of her verging on occasion to near impropriety. Her relationship with her God is, under the textual trappings, quite naive – almost childlike in its innocent desire to please. And this is where there are delightful vignettes of her character drawn by her own pen; she appears quite mercenary over money matters, excess expenditure vexes her, yet, in keeping with the policy of the times and *noblesse oblige* she frequently gives her own money to those in need – but often tempers her obvious reluctance to do so by reminding herself that she is giving it on behalf of her Lord.

Milton House, the family home which Sarah inherited from her father, was a substantial residence standing in some two-and-a-half acres of gardens, paddock and orchard, edging the road in Milton Street and opposite the Baptist Chapel. The sale particulars at the turn of the century describe it as a Family Residence or Hunting Box, and some idea of the size can be gleaned from their details: a sizeable entrance hall, drawing room, dining room, smoking room, billiard room, children's playroom, gun room, china pantry and 'usual offices' on the ground floor, with substantial underground cellars. Ten bedrooms, of which two are servants' dormitories, bathroom, linen cupboard, principal and secondary staircases. Water supply from a never-failing well and 'hot water coils'. The old-fashioned garden is laid out in green walks and arbours and pleasure grounds; a conservatory and two-storied summer house, a well-stocked enclosed kitchen garden, paddock and orchard and stabling for six horses, a large coach house, saddle room and store with overhead loft are approached from the Coronation Street end. A good gardener's cottage adjoins the property.

As with other families of the upper middle-class status, the Thomas household had servants, but the actual staff was very small in number and very much part of the family and privy to much of what was going on. From her entries, Sarah did her full share of household duties and chores and she often showed real concern for her maids' health and spiritual well-being. The responsibilities weighed heavily on Sarah as head of the family home and her dedication to carrying on the spiritual charge and welfare of the members of the Particular Baptist Chapel at Meysey Hampton, which her father built at his own expense in 1845.

Sarah's commitment to the cause reveals an insight into the prejudices and schisms which existed between the denominations in mid-Victorian England, for there are many instances in her entries which point to intransigent rules by which their lives were governed. And yet, there are also several instances when, with great foresightedness for the age, Sarah tried to reconcile those differences in her fundamental and inherent Christian values towards a unity which has only fairly recently been fully explored, developed and accepted. It is also a revelation as to how Milton House was used like the old Mission Houses – as accommodation and stop-over for visiting ministers. At times it would seem that the Thomas's house could hardly be called their own.

Sarah allowed herself some degree of private reflection on her life and position. She clearly wished to be mistress of her own destiny, but felt compelled to await some divine direction as to which path she should follow.

As Sarah opens her diary in 1860 there is already mention of Mr Davis, John or Dear J, according to her mood – a young minister of Arlington Chapel, some six miles distant – and it is obvious that Sarah has romantic feelings for him and he appears not to have hidden his affection for her. He should fulfil all her requirements – a Baptist minister as was her father and grandfather – but she doubts his utter commitment to his calling. He flirts with her friends and her maids in an effort to make her jealous and she tortures herself by weighing up love and loyalty to Dear J and God, to whom she passes on her every problem, whether it be guiding her heart or selecting a suitable housemaid. It is this constant conflict of emotions and conscience that colours the story – a story which acquires a further complication when another suitor re-appears. Meanwhile, punctuating the passage of which, if either, of these two she shall be directed to, Sarah has some rather amusing encounters with other would-be or might-be or could-be suitors before she makes her final choice.

Those secrets have been locked away in a handful of small pocket books for 130 years. Written in a beautiful hand which never altered its style, filling each close line from edge to edge and, on occasion, vertically across the page as well, Sarah made her diaries her closest confidante, silently spelling out her innermost feelings, her prayers, her passion and by so doing penning an intimate picture of her own self and an age which now belongs to the once-upon-a-time. Let us now open those pages ....

1860

❦ JANUARY ❧

Thurs 19th   The day for Kate's return from Bath has come at last. Having prepared everything for the reception of herself and Sarah Wassell and her new fiancé, I was able to leave for Cirencester at 10½, Richard[1] driving the coburg. First called on Mrs Stephens, but only he at home. Met Mrs Sparks and had a long chat with her. Went to bank and found £30 due to Exors account. Met our folks at 2½. Thought Kate looked better than I expected. My first impressions of John Roberts were not prepossessing. We returned to tea at 7 off herring, cake and tongue. All were very tired. Was surprised to notice John Roberts so attentive to my dear Kate, much more so than to his Sarah.

Sun 22nd   Kate feels and looks very poorly again. Sarah, John and I went to church but didn't enjoy Mr Rice's sermon, so we went to Meysey Hampton in the afternoon and to the chapel over the road[2] in the evening. Charles said he would stay home with Kate, I feel much discouraged that she seems not to have improved.

Mon 23rd   Kate too ill to come down, so had a fire in inner bedroom. I sent for Mr Cornwall and he appeared to be concerned that her bowels are so disturbed. John Roberts is more familiar with us than I like and is more attentive to us than to Sarah, so was pleased when he received a letter this morning hastening him back to Bath. He is most sadly disappointed, but not we.

Tues 24th   I went to Cirencester with Sarah and John. She was so curt and queer with him that it sorely vexed me. She says she won't promise to marry him now and many other queer and haughty things. Poor girl, I cannot but pity her for she has much to learn. I was extremely annoyed at John Roberts kissing me when he said goodbye at the station. I had early cup of tea with the Keyworths and reached home at 7. Heard of Mr Brasington's death and Mr Miller's and John Bevin's. Mr Clissold had supper here and spent the night.

Thurs 26th Mr Cornwall[3] called this morning and said he would see Kate in bed tomorrow. Paid bills to John Dance for groceries, Fowlers for brazing the tinware, Wakefields for our drapery stuffs and to Thomas Lea for Charles's tailoring. Mr Clissold came to tea and we had music and singing in the evening. I must not forget to note the prayer meeting last night as it was the first united meeting between the Baptists and Independents. The chapel was full. Mr Clissold went and much enjoyed it. St Mary's Church people are really mortified that 7 or 8 prayers every night were sustained throughout the week, mostly different men each night the week before last, and all of them from the poor despised dissenters. Now, instead of continuing the united meetings once a week as proposed, they wish to meet amongst themselves for prayer. When Mr Lemon comes to lecture on the revivals in Ireland, having been an eye witness, the Rev Mr Rice[4] will devote 3 evenings in the week for united prayer. They meet in Farmor's Schoolroom, but last night schoolmaster Graystone alone prayed.

Fri 27th We all rose at 7, then after breakfast Charles and Mr Clissold started for Nailsworth. The morning was wet. Mr Smith came in to tea after preaching at Meysey Hampton.[5] I had to inform him that we could now raise only £26 a year for his stipend. He received it very nicely and said Meysey Hampton village had much to be grateful for and were greatly indebted to our family as dear Papa had built the chapel there entirely at his own expense. He thought we were most generous and liberal when I gave him 4d to make up 2s 6d church money for Betty Miller, and the same amount for Hannah Vincent, though she be an old busybody and Thomas Woolley. Mr Cornwall examined Kate and said to my joy that he saw no reason why her medical condition should not be soon improving and she should be restored to good health.

Sat 28th This morning had quite a trial to engage in family prayer. Yet I could not neglect it because Charles is out. Called Esther in from the kitchen to participate, though I fear she is still a heathen. Paid Brown, butcher.

Sun 29th Kate up to breakfast, but we had no-one to drive us to M-Hampton and it was too wet to walk, so went over the way. The box for weekly offerings was in use today for the first time. I had nothing but a halfpence to put in. Mr Cornwall called to see Kate in afternoon, he is much cast down over Mr Burke's illness, says he cannot be living now. Mr Frise[6] and she supped here after he had preached a soul-less sermon over the road. Last night at midnight Kate and I much alarmed by a violent knock on the door, Esther came down from the servants' dormitory in sad disarray and frightened. We all clung to each other, Charles being still away, and I offered up a prayer behind the bolted door for we knew 'twas a runaway. I am sure it was not an escapee from the lunatic asylum,[7] though Mr Iles does not manacle them now as once they were. After a while we heard the vagabond run off and Esther was all for making off again to bed when I reminded her that we had to thank our watchful Father for our deliverance.

Mon 30th   A new trial this morning as I had to engage Harriet, who had come in to work, in family prayer, I felt 'twas but a feeble affair so went to prayer meeting in evening but very few were out it being so wet. Even Mr Frise was not there, and he the Minister too. Mr Shepherd told me that Mrs Giles, the chapel cleaner, had told him that she had asked for her husband's conversion, and there was an immediate change came over him.

❧ FEBRUARY ❧

Wed 1st   Harriet came again to work. Charles wrote to say he will return from Cheltenham to Nailsworth in time for the musical entertainment. He says he is well and comfortable. I went with Mrs Frise to the Crofts chapel[8] to hear Mr Shepherd's preaching. I felt quite overcome with a sense of my own deficiencies.

Thurs 2nd   Being quite out of coal and it being frosty weather, I wrote to Uncle Ben Thomas[9] for the horses to go to Cirencester and he would not let me have them, saying he could not find work for the men unless he had the horses. I was very angry, but Mrs Frise and Kate cooled me down and advised my writing a polite note to say I should be obliged if he would try and manage to spare the horses as we are quite out of coal, and if he had any difficulty to find work, Charles would be glad for May to come to complete the job he had started before he left to go to Uncle B.T. Kate thought I should also add that I was under engagement to go to Arlington tomorrow, but I would not do so, knowing how Aunt B.T. would read something into it. The note, written and approved by both Kate and Mrs Frise, was sent. But my anger was renewed when it met with no success at all.

Fri 3rd   The ground slightly covered with snow, but the sun shone and I managed to borrow a horse for Richard to drive me to Arlington. Belchers were glad to see me. Mr Frise came over for dinner but had to hurry off to tune another piano, I had to ask the Lord's forgiveness in private as I thought to myself that he would make a better tuner of pianos than minister of souls. Mr Davis came to tea. He was up for fun and he, Hannah, Olivia and I had quite a game. He was very attentive and pressed me much to stay to prayer meeting and I yielded reluctantly as I had quite a pain in the heart and was anxious about Kate left at home, but after a glass of brandy and a slice of bread and butter, was quite revived. The horse ran back, nearly over the bank on our return and quite upset me. I was obliged to get out of the coburg and walk down the hill. Mr Davis then joined me, quite to my surprise and I felt quite agitated. It was a beautiful moonlight night and he tied his pony to the back of the coburg to ride inside with me. He said the influence of someone close to him made him very merry. My palpitations returned and I tried to resort to private prayer, alas, I feel, without much success in it. Was pleased to find Kate a little better on my return and she had not thought me long away. Mr and Mrs Rice had called. Sorry to have missed them, as I do feel it would be Christian to make more contact with the church priest, though we do

Milton Street, Fairford showing Sarah Thomas's house on the far right

not always agree with their way of reaching our Eternal Father. There is every likelihood of Mr Rice succeeding to the baronetcy of Dynevor. Mrs Rice left us her copy of The Life of Mrs Winslow. Received a letter from John Roberts addressed C.J. Kingsley, so could not open it until Charles's return, though Kate thought I could being head of the household. I was quite shocked that she should say that Charles was 'but our half brother', but she repented and we engaged together in private prayer.

Mon 6th B.T. did not send for our coal until Saturday. Invited to tea at Frises, but Kate afraid of the cold. Charles returned from his visit to Nailsworth, which he enjoyed. He said he was shocked at the manner in which the young Clissolds treat their parents. It was very nice to have him home again and he is glad to come. He said he settled with Mullings for the Pest House[10] at Burdocks as he came through Cirencester. Charles kindly drove me to the turning at Meysey Hampton and I visited the sick and also the school, though I felt most unwell, but feel that I am obliged to carry on these duties for dear Papa's sake. Left some tracts at Clarks, but the Edwards not at home. Had close conversation with Miller's wife and looked in on Haywards. Fear old Woolly does not fully understand the plague of his own heart. Poor Ecott, too, I fear is in darkness, though she hopes to be saved and seemed grateful for my visit, but whether for the salvation of her soul or the sustenance of the port wine I took her, only God can say. Mrs Bedwell, kind biddy as ever, made me tea. I ran in to see Kitty Price (Hart) for the first time since her marriage. At Trumans I left some meat and two fresh laid eggs at Lovedays, and was thus enabled to speak earnestly to her. I was anxious not to hear any gossip anywhere – though there is much abroad. Richard walked over to walk back with me, it being quite dark after I had been to Framptons and Giles Vincent's.

Wed 8th Called on Mrs Lane, they asked me to stay tea and offered cake and wine. I refused the former and accepted the latter, then remembered on my way back that it could have been wedding cake that I had declined, but they did not produce it in time. Called on Miss Wise and Miss Iles. Ran up to Mrs Savory's with the basket she had left behind. He is in London and she seems much more herself when he is not there, fears he dwells too much in the past and the damage done to the machinery[11] out on the green in the riots here, though Charles points out the harshness of the sentences on those who broke up the machinery and many local men will never return from transportation for it. However, Mrs S is a good friend and neighbour to us. Did some gardening for the first time this year. Transplanted roses with Richard's help into our new border. Then Richard and May removed gooseberry trees.

Sat 11th The snow fell thick and fast for a couple of hours, we've not had it so wintery before this season. Went to read to Mrs Dickson, but it was not convenient, so went to Abram Cowley instead, but he would keep interrupting my reading as he is suffering much in his bowels recently. He says he is grateful to God for putting kindness in our hearts for him, so I suppose I must suffer his sufferings with him. I read him Mr Spurgeon's farewell sermon in the Music Hall. I shall endeavour to send it to Mr Davis without his knowing where it comes from, for I feel he might also profit from it. Charles baptizing announced for next Sunday evening.

Mon 13th Hard frost again, so slippery yesterday that we could not get to Meysey Hampton. Miss Iles from Park Corner school[12] said her young ladies were delighted with the snow. She came alone to Dorcas[13] meeting.

Tues 14th Valentine's Day, but the only letter we had was one for Kate from Miss Attwater. Then a vexatious circumstance occurred this afternoon in which I considered Kate to be in the wrong and I felt inclined to resent it. I went to chapel and there all naughty feelings were suddenly dispelled and I was enabled to go home with a smiling face and kindly feelings. Called on old Thomas Simpson and Susan Cowly.

Wed 15th Expected friends from Arlington but they did not come. Mr and Mrs Nicholas came this morning without my having left a calling card – found out later they are Unitarian. Mr Stephens called for tea, but stayed and supped and slept here. He was full of spirits.

Fri 17th Had bacon pig killed – 11 score 13lb. Snow vanished yesterday.

Sun 19th Took little Jesse Frise with me to Meysey Hampton, he was very good. The chapel was crowded. Sam Reid and Edward Smith baptized.

Mon 20th Had nice long letter from Mr King and one from Mrs King. Frise came over in afternoon and did not need pressing to stay tea. Charles had three extra pipes while Frise was here and when he left went to Uncle Ben Thomas though 'twas late. He did not return until the clock struck midnight, then wanted another pipe but we had put it all away. He became very cross because we didn't give him any more tobacco and he wouldn't go to bed. Kate and I sat upstairs listening for him until after 1 o'clock, then tired and sad we got into bed.

Tues 21st   I went down determined so make the peace with Charles, having asked God's guidance in the matter as Kate and Charles were quite annoyed with each other – but then it was alright, so after dinner I put pipe and tobacco ready for him. I fear Frise is not a goodly influence to him. This is Shrove Tuesday and we had much fun tossing pancakes.

Wed 22nd   Very unwell. Throat so painful I could hardly talk to Mr Cornwall when he called to see Kate. Mr Smith tead here and Charles paid him for preaching at Meysey Hampton, £10.

Thurs 23rd   Breakfasted in bed, still being unwell. Prayed alone and put my troubles before Our Lord, especially in respect of dear J. This I learnt from reading Mrs Winslow, that when she prayed for her unconverted children or friends her prayers were often answered in a most remarkable way. Mr Cornwall sent some tincture with his servant for my mouth.

Tues 28th   I went to Cirencester to meet Mr Wassell. As the wind blew a hurricane yesterday Mrs Belcher had to stay the night as she could not walk home in it to Bibury. She came with me and we took scrap dinner at Keyworths.[16] I took Charles's book to the bank and ran around doing some errands.

Wed 29th   Leap Year Day. This has been a day of bustle. Mr Frise came and sat some time and hindered somewhat, then Mrs Sparks called. After dinner Susan Cornwall came and directly after she left Mrs Radway, Ellen Booker, who was quite agreeable today, and Ellen Yells called. I was pleased to see the latter, not knowing she was in the neighbourhood. They stayed tea then we went to Crofts chapel and they returned here to sup.

❦ MARCH ❧

Thurs 1st   The whole day I was obliged to rest as still very unwell. Mr Cornwall called and confirmed that I am not well, advised brandy and water and a return to bed. Kate a little better.

Fri 2nd   This day brings our dear Papa to mind very strongly, this being his birthday. How differently we are circumstanced now. Last year it was a most distressing day. He had become so delirious in the night that I had to run at 4 o'clock in the morning to Dr Page and he gave him such a strong dose of opium that he slept most fearfully throughout the day and Dr Page could not rouse him. But now he is beyond all suffering and delivered from the infirmities of this life and is now turning his praises to an endless eternity.

Sat 3rd   Feeling better I went to Cirencester with Mr Wassell.[14] He hasn't been in good spirits, and now mine are far from good having heard from Charles that he, Mr W, had asked for £5 towards his expenses, though Charles paid everything whenever they went to town. He also borrowed 26 shillings. I think him very mean because Charles had already told him that he would take nothing for his expenses and he should therefore take nothing for his. Wassell knows how we are all pressed just now, and all he says is 'I know it has been a tremendous time for you all.' All this after I had paid him £2 on my return home, not knowing of it all. He said he thought he ought not to take it, but did. And he married to a wife with £30,000. Glad when he returns home.

Sun 4th   Went to see old Abram, but he was too much in suffering to concentrate on anything but his bowels. I had prepared 'The blood of Jesus ...' so left the place marked for him, though I know not whether he can read. Sent him a poached egg by Esther.

Mon 5th   Have been sorely tried today. A woman came to say she heard my servant was leaving and she came to offer her daughter. When I asked Esther about it she instantly said 'Oh, it's a mistake, I've said nothing about it.' Then, after a while she said she was going to leave. It was like a thunderclap to me, as I'd no idea of it. I asked her reasons and she said 'twas different to what she had been used to. She was alone here and had always been a servant where there were several. I asked if she had any complaints against us and she said No, but she didn't like going to chapel. I told her she was acting very unhandsomely, and should have named it to me. I put it to Our Lord at the prayer meeting when I privately asked Him His guidance in this matter, though I fear Esther had done herself no good in not wishing to meet Him at chapel and always felt that she did not fully engage at family prayer at home with us as a good servant should.

Tues 6th Was surprised to hear that Ann had left Miller because she had scarletina, especially as she had nursed him through it, and probably had caught it from him. 'Tis singular she should be out of a place just as Esther is going, but I don't think it would be well to have her again, but cannot decide this thing for myself alone as I have not heard from God the direction He would point out to me. Jane Burrows from Coln came to offer herself, but I could see she wouldn't suit. I called on Mrs Reynolds and was appalled to hear that Mrs Vines had boxed Sarah's ears in the street for not being home sooner from singing class. Salmon went to the asylum to report that one of the patients had escaped, he had noticed him as he was dealing with the beer dray and could tell he was a lunatic. The Keeper came out to look round our garden and orchard just in case he was hiding there, poor wretch.

Wed 7th Have been very sadly all day. Hated myself and am grieved I get so easily ruffled as Kate and I were with each other last night. Spoke again to Esther and she said it was so dull here. I said I was sorry she was not comfortable with us and she should talk it over with her mother. Charles went to Meysey Hampton and accompanied Smith, who is too feeble to go alone to get the folks to sign a petition against church rates. Mr and Mrs Hewer and Mr Lytton signed. Mr Hobbs was out. Tovey sat pen in hand to sign, but his wife would not let him. Charles had long argument with her and found her very ignorant.

Thurs 8th Shopped at Dances for stationery and coming across the Market Place met Miss Iles. Was very struck with Mrs Winslow's old John Newton saying 'If the buzzing of a fly is an annoyance to us, it is our privilege to carry it to Jesus'. I indeed find it to be so, and shall continue to put this problem of the servant to Him as such a privilege.

Fri 9th Lo and behold, Esther said that she had last evening spoken to her mother on her situation here and her mother wouldn't advise her one way or the other. I find it to be a trial and it drives me to prayer. I have now asked Him to direct Esther as to what is right for us, for I shall regret her going as she suits us nicely and I know it doesn't happen by chance. Sam Burge and Mrs came in to sup. I took an unwanted petticoat to Widow Sly. She's lost her husband 6 weeks now. I then visited Widow Davis, she wept much when she talked of her little girl that died so happy.

Sat 10th Kate and I posted letters to William and John;[15] it is now 11 months since I heard from John and feel they should show more concern for us, their sisters. They had all the land and houses in Fairford, except this one, which is mine, left to them by dear Papa, yet they show not the slightest interest in it or us. I fear they have not sought Christianity in the way dear Papa brought us up to. I fail to understand it, and have written just so to them on it. Snow all afternoon and winterly cold. Kate has had much trouble with her bowels all week. Prayed earnestly for dear J. I cannot forget him. When, dear Lord, will Thou answer my prayers for him.

Mon 12th Received dividend warrant £12 10s on English and Australian copper shares. At Dorcas evening, Miss Iles gave me a bottle of ginger wine to bring home for Kate.

Wed 14th Was discouraged this morning as we had no servant in view then felt reproved when a good-tempered looking girl from Paynes came to offer. She had been there 3 years and looked a likely one. Mrs Keyworth[16] had come by carrier cart from Cirencester and so to Arlington with me. As we got out at the mill we could hear the piano being played. It was Mr Davis teaching Mary Anne. He returned later to tea with us and afterwards we had some music, which was most enjoyable then he was obliged to to take the singing class. I could see Miss Hatton's eye on him and his on me and Mrs Belcher watching us both. She later asked if Mr Davis could walk over with her and Mr Short to us on Friday.

Thurs 15th Kate feeling better came with us to tea and sup at Frises over the way. Charles also came to sup. The chairs and table were filthy, they could not have been dusted for days. We were obliged to wipe the chairs with some needlework which Mrs Frise had given me to do before we could sit down. Poor Mrs Keyworth said she had never seen anything equal to it in her life, not even in the meanest cottage, sad! sad!

Fri 16th Prevailed on Mrs Keyworth to stay another day. Mrs

Belcher, Mary Anne and Mr Davis walked in through the garden at 1 o'clock. I was cleaning the parlour window and pretended not to see him. I wore my hair rolled for the first time. Mr Davis was too full of fun and I did not enjoy it in front of company. I had to coax him to go to prayer meeting. Mrs Burge and Bessie Coles came to tea, then it rained so hard the Arlington friends couldn't walk home, so we had to prepare beds for them, and as if that were not enough, Frise and Sam Burge came in to sup.

Sat 17th Mrs Keyworth left by Collett by cart again. Kate came with me for the ride when I took the Arlington friends home. My mind is perplexed about Mr Davis. I thought I liked him, but I fear his trifling will be of no help to me, but his thoughts are obviously directed to me, and all are hinting at it. Sent Francis to tell Paynes servant to call as she left on Tuesday. Mr Smith called to ask if Scoble could take the Meysey Hampton service, but as he had already been paid for it we thought not. We shall go over the way to hear him at Fairford.

Sun 18th Scoble and several high folks at chapel. Ann Mitchell, silly girl, was quite excited about it. We were much alarmed to hear of the fire at Arlington. It was said 18 ricks of Mr Groves's were on fire. A great many folks from Fairford went over to see it, and I caught one to take a note to Mrs Belcher to enquire as to the truth of it.

Mon 19th Kate and I called on Susan Cornwall and vexed to find that when the maid brought Jim's dinner in he would not come in for it as we were there.

Tues 20th Had long account from Mrs Belcher on the fires. Only 4 or 5, not 18 ricks had been burned, but she said as how Mr Dutton from the Court worked hard between two poor men. Mr Davis, too, she said got ladies even to form a rank to pass the buckets of water. I was not surprised to hear that he had stayed to do so thus missing taking his evening service, no doubt his congregation understood the reason.

Fri 23rd It has been a sad blustering day. This day week the first message was received by the Indian telegraph that the Redgauntlet had been burnt. The curious fact is that though the first news flashed along the great cable of 3,000 miles from Kurrachee to Alexandria should be that of a disabled Atlantic line – the record of a shipping disaster.

Sat 24th   Charles went to Down Ampney to get more names to petition for the abolition of church rates. Frise is so cowardly, he won't take his petition to Ferris though Charles told him that he made him promise to sign it. He seems frightened of him being a farmer, but he won't take it to any of the church people either. Then Frise came to sup and said Mr Davis was going to Swindon with him on Good Friday and would want a bed here.

Tues 27th   Kate and I made the long dreaded visit to Mrs Rice to return her book. But she was quite affable. Mr Rice was still preaching at St Mary's so we did not see him.

Wed 28th   Went to Cirencester and registered at Comleys for a servant. Was told they would send one to be seen after dinner, we arranged to see her at our friends, the Keyworths. She arrived and seemed likely to suit but did not leave Capt Hickman's until 20th April.

Bought rose tree at the nursery, then called at bank for books. It was shut up but Mr Creese and Edgehill were there. Mr Creese said I had to sign my name and Kate must do so before she could draw a cheque. We supped at Keyworths then returned after George Clissold had left home.

Thurs 29th   Kate asked Esther if she would mind staying until 20th as we had not heard of a servant who could come before then, but she declined though she owned she had no place in view. We thought it unkind of her. I am very discouraged as I had made this a subject of prayer and it seems God has not heard me. Kate is quite knocked up from the exertions of our trip to town yesterday and I nearly so, but more so from the prospect before us of no servant. Susan Cornwall came to tea and they had another trouble – Mrs Jones is now without a home and is expecting her sons home from sea. We then talked over our love affairs.

Fri 30th   I had asked Susan to ask her father to call on Kate, but we saw him pass the door and stayed in for him, but he did not call. H. Brown came to say she couldn't come for more than to sleep and to attend to selling milk. Again this is vexatious.

Sat 31st   Esther worked hard to near 10 this evening and nicely cleaned up all the places and then left. Before she went I urged upon her the necessity of seeking salvation and she seemed to feel it. I have always prayed for her conversion and trust these prayers will not be in vain. Mr Painter came in evening to smoke with Charles.

APRIL

Sun 1st Harriet Brown came to sleep last night, she rose and prepared room for us. This morning I escaped from what might have been a serious accident. Having gone into stable to feed the pet lambs with milk, I turned hastily and my foot slipped and I fell with great force on my temple. Luckily Charles heard me cry out and came to assist me get up. My face instantly swelled and dear Kitty, ever kind, washed the mud and

blood from my face and badly cut knee. It gave me a sad shake, and I felt the effects of it throughout the day. Kate and I have surpassed ourselves on this April fool's day – me by striking my head and Kate by ringing the bell for Esther.

Mon 2nd Mr Cornwall called this morning. I asked him seriously about Kate's recovery chances and he thought they were quite good, but it is a tedious case, but considers that she is mending. I am thankful for that but am distressed about its continuance. Charles bought a pretty iron garden chair this morning to stand on the lawn.

Tues 3rd Finding I could have the horse, I dined at 12 and rode to Cirencester to settle finally with the servant who came to see me at Keyworths. She gave me the good news that her master had said they were not intending to keep so many servants again and she might leave at once if she liked. After tea Mrs Keyworth and Hannah went with me to do my errands.

Thurs 5th Mr Cornwall called again, but of course, Kate is better today. We get on very comfortably with Harriet.

Good Friday   Mr Davis came about 10 o'clock. After lunch he went with Frise to Swindon, having hired Dance's trap. They returned about 10. I spent an hour this afternoon in earnest prayer asking Our Lord to grant wisdom and skill to Mr Cornwall to find out Kate's malady and to direct him to prescribe something for her good, and to give me patience to await the outcome of this entreaty.

Sat 7th   Mrs Rose came to clean up. Harriet helps us nicely in the mornings. Was much surprised on answering the door to see Ann Laight. Poor girl. I was grieved to see how she looked so thin and ill and she could eat nothing. I boiled her an egg and gave her brandy and water, but she couldn't eat the egg. I made her stay the night and she slept with Harriet, then she would get to work and help Mrs Rose to clean up. Mr Davis still here. He begins to show signs of great interest in me and when we were alone he told me how much he loved me, but I would not let him talk of it and I felt quite unwell over it during the evening and had to lie on the sofa.

Sun 8th   Mr Davis preached for Mr Frise and Kate went over the way to hear him. They brought little Jesse Frise over with them to dinner and having the child here seemed to make Mr Davis long to have one of his own. He made me feel very awkward sometimes. He, Charles and I went to Meysey Hampton in the afternoon and Mr Davis administered the ordinance, speaking very faithfully and affectionately to the members. I enjoyed the service more than usual. Charles took Jesse into the vestry and Mr Davis had much fun over him being naughty there and generally misbehaving. In the evening we three went to chapel over the way and Kate stayed home, Ann staying to read to her.

Mon 9th   Mr Davis still being here, I tried to get Mrs Bedwell to come in to cook for us, but she was ill. I then tried Suky, she was out as was Sarah Davis. At last I obtained Ruth Ballinger. She stayed until the servant arrived and was much pleased with the shilling I gave her for her services. I offered Harriet 5 shillings, but she positively refused more than 3 shillings.

Tues 10th   Susan Cornwall called this afternoon to ask us to go to church bazaar at Lechlade on Thursday. Mr Davis was at Frises so she didn't know he was here. Her papa has had a fall and hurt his foot so that he cannot walk as far as this yet. Mr Davis was to have returned to his service this evening, but jumped up at tea, looked at his watch and found he would be too late for it. I thought him very naughty not to go to chapel. I went without him for my heart was heavy and I thought the house of God was the best place to go for relief. Mr Davis had spoken freely of his position and made me acquainted with his wishes respecting myself and thus is the cause of my anxiety. While at chapel the text of 'Be careful for nothing' seemed to ring true for me. I am in a difficulty. I feel that I have some regard for him and yet I don't think it would be a suitable union. I wait direction from my Heavenly Father. Mr Frise came in to sup and Mr Davis was much taken to, as he didn't want Frise to know that he had stayed and missed chapel.

Wed 11th Mr Davis left at 4½. I was much surprised to see how much he felt at home with me and conversed very familiarly on many things (inter alias a la Kidd). He says he is in expectation of moving from his position as minister at Arlington chapel and would seek a place where his income would allow him to provide a home for me. I begged him not to think of me in that way. I told him honestly that I foresaw many difficulties in the way, though I could not tell him what they were. He then asked if there was anyone else in my life to cause an impediment to his desire, but I would not satisfy him, simply that I had no confidence in my own judgment and this was such a serious matter that I could not take steps towards marriage until I could see that Providence had so directed my steps. He then said that he too would make it a matter of prayer. He wished to begin a correspondence, but I declined it, so he said he would come over again very soon. Our new maid does not seem so cleanly as Esther and appears rather raw-boned, but she desires to please and has done the lambs' tails, cleaning and skinning them well enough, so we had them fried in egg and breadcrumbs after Kate and I had shown her how to do them. Mr Frise came in at 7 to say that a Mr Whitlock, a Baptist Minister of East Combe near Stroud had just come to his house and would need a bed for the night. Knowing that Frise's is rather unsavoury, Kate and I told him that if he would accept Mr Davis's bed just as he left it, he should be welcome to it, but we did not have time to change the sheets for him. He was pleased with it. He is collecting for the Scholastic Institution at Birmingham for the sons of ministers.

Thurs 12th Alas, I do not feel greatly prepossessed with our new maid. I pray that she'll do better by and bye. Mr Whitlock left this morning. The weather is still wet and cold.

Sat 14th   It is thought advisable that I should go to London and meet Wassell either at Swindon or Faringdon Road. I seek direction from above as I am not able to decide upon anything myself, but I fear Kate is not well enough to go.

Sun 15th   Frise preached at Meysey Hampton. He said he thought Kate is in a very poor low way and it distresses me to hear people say so, many glanced anxiously at her as we went across to chapel in the evening. When we returned Charles told me that he had written to Capt Milbourne.

Mon 16th   Charles went to Cirencester with Uncle B.T. After dinner Kate and I went down to Cornwalls, and I asked him about Kate going to London. He said that he supposed I was taking the opportunity to seek further advice on her condition from a London doctor and he looked quite jealous as he spoke. The fact is I feel he is jealous of her going and doing so. It stung me to hear him say so and I had to have some brandy and sugar to revive me. I saw Kate indoors on our return then ran to Miss Inmans to sympathise about Betterton. He died at the orphan asylum in London and his friends feel it deeply. Then I visited Abram Cowley, Polly Woodman and Sarah Westbury, stayed long with the latter as she is very anxious about her soul, so I feel much interest in her.

Wed 18th   Had but little sleep, my heart is heavy with anxiety about Kate. I feel most unfit for my journey. I would love to shed tears but dare not give way as I should betray myself and my inner fears to my dear Kitty, the object of my sadness. At Cirencester I stayed a while with Mrs Keyworth, ever kind she made me lie down upstairs as she could see I was distressed, had a little doze and cry then as I rose the first thing I saw on going to the window was the churchyard burial ground. It was a dismal sight in my frame of mind and then I could not help but think of what Richard had said a week or so back while he was helping in the garden. He said there were two ravens flying over the garden that morning, cawing all the way, and it made him quite low as it was a sign of death. It was a foolish thing for me to think of it, but I could not banish it from my thoughts, though I don't believe in it. Mr Belcher came in with his two children and he came with me to station, felt uneasy about starting me off as we did not know if Wassell would meet me at Swindon. However, he did, and so I travelled with him to Wantage. A young woman on the train asked after 'the other Miss Thomas,' but it turned out to be Esther

Burge. Mr Wassell reached our destination at 9 and had tea and egg. I then wrote home in a more cheerful strain than I really felt.

Thurs 19th Mr Wassell left this morning when Mr Moses came to introduce himself. I felt rather awkward on hearing that young Walduck had lost father, wife and child and that the only females in the house beside myself were two domestic servants. Mr Walduck waited upon us and the gents were very polite.

Fri 20th Wassell called for me and we dined at an eating house in Holborn and I bought a trunk for 15 shillings. Went with Thurston[17] to pay £11 12s. 10d into Masterman's Bank to be remitted to our account at Gloucester Bank at Cirencester, then returned to mope about until time for tea at Randall's. Met Msr Robineau from Paris there, also Mr Jenkins, his interpreter and Mr Jenkins's daughter. Felt much interest in Msr Robineau on hearing of his suffering for conscience sake. He has been turned out of the reformed church in Paris for embracing baptist views and for admitting to being baptised. He is in England collecting money to build a chapel. Had supper with Mr Wassell at Warwick Court.

Sat 21st Walduck showed me all over the house this morning and then I left for South Street. After dinner went to soirée at Regent Park College. I was much struck with the splendour of the building. We were shown into a large handsome room to take off our wrappers, then being late, taken into the coffee room at once and were waited on by Mr Williams, a young student who afterwards took me over the college and was anxious for me to see his own study, but I ventured not further than the door, being quite alone with him by that time. He secured me a good seat for the lectures and showed me the relics of Carey's signboard. I felt quite took to on seeing Mr and Mrs Pearce and daughter, it bringing the time so vividly to mind when my precious mother and I and Mrs Clarke and Sophy tead at their house in Romford. It was most interesting to hear the accounts that the missionaries gave of their labours. First a missionary from Sweden, then Robineau from Paris – but he had to give his lecture in French and Mr Jenkins interpreted for him, then one from China who brought with him a native Christian and a missionary from Canada. Robineau, Jenkins and Mr Yates accompanied me to the station but we lost our way and only caught the last train as it was pulling out. Msr Robineau badly wants to come to Fairford, having heard my speaking of it – at least through his interpreter – and the ministry which dear Papa founded at Meysey Hampton.

Mon 23rd   The wet and bitterly cold weather continues. Heard from Kate and Charles. Kate still sadly. Kidd[18] came for me at 11 and asked me to go and choose a kitchen range with him at Deane's. Randall had told him that I was in town. He came everywhere with me. We went by cab to Deane's as it was still wet. He is furnishing a house at White Hall, having left the bank. Having chosen the range, he made me choose a knife for Kate which cost 4/2d, and bought me a pretty fruit knife for 12/-. Then we went to large hotel at London Bridge and insisted I take two large glasses of port wine. We sat a long time by enormous fire. He then put me in a cab, we drove to Fenchurch Station, where he got out, then he paid the driver to take me on to South Street.

Wed 25th   Yesterday being so wet, stayed indoors all day writing. This morn being fine I sallied off to Islington, met with friends and Wassell met up later with us and escorted me home.

Sat 28th   The past few days busy catching up with friends and gossip, and attended chapel service and lectures. Mr Wassell left for Bath today. I felt quite dull when he left, especially as he said he didn't think Sarah's wedding would now take place. At 12 I went to Randalls, and chatted in French to Msr Robineau. Kidd didn't come until after 1. Miss Waskett and I waited for him in the drawing room, then he and I went to Peckham. He made me take a glass of wine with him and took me to Shoreditch after tea. I put some tracts in my pocket before leaving. Two men had been talking in a somewhat off-hand manner and a jocular man who sat over his glass till his train was gone came to our carriage and asked them how best he could leap over the next hour. One of the men advised him that he could do no better than going to the White Hart and having a glass or two. I wished sadly to give him a tract, but for a long time fear hindered my intent, then I prayed to be enabled to do it. At last, after two had got out of the carriage and I was getting out at Waltham, he refused to open the door for me and I said, 'please allow me to give you a tract.' 'Will I allow you,' he said, smiling, 'I suppose it won't do me any harm'. I said, 'No, and my prayer is that it may do you much good, so please read it.' He said, 'I suppose you mean it well.' 'Yes, indeed I do,' I said and shook his hand as I left the train although my knees were shaking, too.

Sun 29th   Have bad cold and feel quite poorly. Harriet asked if she might light a fire in my room, and she was allowed to.

Mon 30th   A fine and warm day, but still feeling effects of my cold. Heard from dear Kate. Mrs Murch called and she asked me to tea, but not as though she meant it, so didn't go. Harriet tends my needs nicely and came with me to Mrs William Websters. I supped at the Pugh's. Thought Mr Pugh was rather fresh.

MAY

Tues 1st   My cold very bad, I enjoy the large fire in my bedroom. My voice was gone for several hours. Left our kind friends Richardson at 11½. Walter walked with me to the station and carried my bag.

Liked Ed very much. They are all nice boys. Weather very warm today. Got out at Stratford and having to wait a long time wrote in pencil to dear Kate to say I should be home on Thursday.

I reached Grays at 3 and found Kidd waiting for me. He took me to his house in a brougham. I posted my letter at Grays. Saw a heron and many partridges on the way down. Kidd showed me all over the house and round the garden. He has had a vast number of trees of all kinds planted and he has furnished the house very nicely. At one of the windows, standing to look out at the garden, I painted the whole front of my crepe skirt and dress, but Kidd got me some turpentine and it was alright. For some time he declared I should stay the night, but seeing I was very determined, said it was alright that I should go. He then rang for the servant to bring me some nice hot coffee and bread and butter and then went for brougham. The horse galloped all the way as the man said it was a near go and this was the last train home tonight. Kidd put me in first class carriage and I reached my lodgings safely just after 10, very tired.

Wed 2nd   I went to Randalls at 10. Kidd arrived from Grays and went with me to Savorys for watch and I paid 7/- for it. We then went to Hitchcocks and bought sleeves and cuffs for Hannah and a collar for dear Kate. Kidd then took me all round St Paul's and we walked back to Worseys to a good dinner. He rested on the sofa and left at 5, having to go to an evening party. Had there been time he wanted me to go with him to order his wedding suit. He talks of coming to Fairford soon, but as he is to marry shortly he cannot give a date. That is, as he says, if it doesn't fall through as it has often done before. Mrs B begged me to go to tea as she had something to say to me. When alone, after tea, she told me that Mr Williams of the Regents Park College spent last Sunday there and preached at their Welsh chapel. He enquired particularly after me and wished her to present to me his very kind regards. He told her that he wished he had a friend to confide in, and make a bosom friend of, and none had come so near to his choice as myself, saying he had been much struck with me the day at the soireée. I could not but feel amused, but though he is a nice fellow and his appearance much resembles that of Mr East, he must be several years younger than I am and that in itself would be a barrier to anything more than friendship. Msr Robineau expected his uncle from Paris today, but had hoped to accompany me part of the homeward journey, but as he is to meet with Msr Monod tonight that may not be possible. They are to meet with the French prostitutes and Msr Robineau is to address them. However, he returned at 11, saying that his uncle had not arrived and he was reluctant to attend the meeting alone with the prostitutes he would await his uncle's arrival and follow on Friday. Mr Jenkins, his interpreter, would not be needed for the meeting so he would leave London tomorrow as arranged. Unfortunately I was late returning and through misunderstanding my bed was let. However, Miss Spicer kindly gave me half her bed, and I quite liked her. Had a chat with Miss Waskett and Townley Clarke at Randalls. Poor Townley has an affection of the brain so that she cannot raise open her eyelids and it is the doctor's opinion that she'll never be any better. I felt thankful that they don't say so with regard to my dear Kate.

Thurs 3rd   The little stamp case that I had missed was not found and I have felt great annoyance at it, having hunted all my places for it. At 9 Mr Jenkins and I started for home. He seemed to feel vexed that Msr Robineau didn't come too. We took our tickets to Didcot second class and then had but 11 minutes to get tickets third class to Cirencester and Bristol and to see to luggage, but did it comfortably. At Swindon I parted with Mr Jenkins and reached Keyworths in Cirencester just before 3. Mrs Keyworth came with me to tea at the Stephens's and I left some of the appeals from Msr Robineau. Left for home at 6½, though they all pressed me to stay to the baptising of Miss Clapham, but I was eager to see dear Kate again, she, too, was delighted that I was home.

Fri 4th   I was extremely tired with travelling and kind Hannah Harris brought us up our breakfasts in bed. Mr Cornwall had seen Kate yesterday and said he thought there was some improvement in her. She seems cheerful and comfortable today. Charles and Kate say I am thinner than before I left home. Elizabeth[19] is so kind to dear Kate. I have more confidence in her than I had in Esther. Miss Wise came and sat some time with us.

Sun 6th   Hannah and I went to Arlington this afternoon, Richard driving. I was so glad Mr D wasn't at Belchers. After the service he didn't come to speak very soon, we just shook hands and I followed Mrs Belcher, but he came down later and rode part of the way home with us and walked back. My mind seems fixed to think nothing of him for since I came home Hannah told me of the affair with him and Ellen Coles in the chapel. His people were greatly annoyed with him for not returning to his service or telling him he would not be there. Consequence was, the people met and dispersed without any service at all. It was when he was here with me on Easter Tuesday. These things will do him harm and he will soon lose all weight and influence with his people. He said he leaves home on Wednesday. I expect he is going somewhere on probation. He is to either make very sure of me or is very indifferent as to the result. He said nothing about coming to see me before he goes, but whichever way it is, it won't do for me. I cannot and do not love him.

Tues 8th   Kate very languid. Frise came to ask me to go to the opening of the Ebenezer Chapel[20] and I went with Mrs Frise and Mr Frise, and Charles. It was crowded. Cowley gave an account of his own experiences and was evidently embarrassed having to speak to so many. Mrs Hewer and Mrs Lytton came to tea, but they thought I looked more ill than Kate does. Her bowels are not so disturbed today.

Thurs 10th   This has been a wet evening. Richard drove me to Coln to pay for flour at the millers and I ordered some more. I asked about my dahlias at the gardeners and he said they were all dead. When I returned I went to Miss Inmans to see if she had brought me the anchovies from London. Called at Iles's to know about the next Dorcas meeting.

Sat 12th   Mr Ferris came from Bristol and after tea he and Charles went out to get subscribers. Kate and I gave 10/- each. Mr Cornwall called but was rather grumpy. Msr Robineau wrote to me in French this morning to say that he would be coming next week and begged me to give all particulars about the journey to here for him. I do not

The Old Smithy, Coln St Aldwyns

consider myself a first-rate scholar in French, so I wrote one letter in French and another in English after much deliberation.

Tues 15th   Kate not so well, but cheerful and patient. Mr Coles called and smoked with Charles and I was busy gardening most of the afternoon.

Wed 16th   Couldn't go to the united meeting at chapel as we had such a teaze with the churning and couldn't leave it.

Thurs 17th   Kate very poorly. I am sad and melancholy. She could not get up until tea-time and then could eat nothing. I gave her hot gin and water, nutmeg and cinnamon at 11 and some more at 3. It seemed to do her more good than Mr Cornwall's medicine. I bought her a pair of soles and some shrimps, but she could only manage half a sole. She then had such a violent headache and rheumatic pains I soaked her feet in warm water with vinegar. Had a letter from Msr Robineau to say he would be here tomorrow, but feels great difficulty in travelling alone as he cannot speak any English at all.

Fri 18th   Heard twice from Msr Robineau. The first to postpone his visit until Saturday, the second to say he could not come now as he thought he must go to Scotland first. It is a great relief to me that he not coming as Kate needs all my ministrations.

Sat 19th Called Mr Cornwall to see Kate as she is so sick and giddy and in violent pain. Charles asked him seriously about her condition and he spoke encouragingly, but now says he would be willing for us to call in Dr Evans although he would obviously prefer for us to be going on as we are. He thought Kate's case was not incurable. Mrs Miller brought her a small trout for her supper.

Mon 21st We have had much kindness, Mrs Savory and Mrs Burge both brought trout for Kate and Mrs Frise and Mrs Iles called to see her. Then to my surprise, Uncle Ben Thomas actually called and brought Kate some brandy as she doesn't like what Charles bought for her, though 'twas the very best pale. Poor, dear girl. She is very ill and I sometimes think she is sinking. The thought of losing her weighs heavily upon me and I can only resort to prayer for strength. I can now find no pleasure in the garden or anything else. I seek for grace for tis very difficult to keep from repining and murmuring. Indeed I cannot always. Dear Charles tries to cheer me up all he can for he thinks me looking very sadly and fears I grieve too much.

Wed 23rd Mr Cornwall has called every day, but today not in his best mood. He agreed to write to Dr Evans tonight, but he didn't seem pleased to do so, though he wouldn't own it. Bessie Booker called and said how plump Kate looked in bed. Stupid woman. She seemed under restraint.

Fri 25th Kate seems a little better today though she still complains of throbbing in the head that it reminds of dear Papa. Mrs Miller sent her some asparagus and Aunt B.T. some jelly and sweetbreads, which she enjoyed.

Sat 26th Kate seems too excitable. Mr Cornwall called to say that Dr Evans would be here at $5\frac{1}{2}$ and we had to break it to Kate as we had not told her of it. She did not like it at first. They arrived an hour later than arranged and after Dr Evans had warmed his hands at the fire we all went to the sick room and he made Kate tell her own tale. She answered every question with composure. The two doctors went downstairs to consult privately then returned to tell the treatment. Dr Evans said that she was appearing to have a succession of small blisters on the tender part of the bowels. By no means was she to take aperient medicine, but a little salad oil or lemon juice when necessary. She was not to let the bowels go over two days without moving and to use an enema with $\frac{1}{2}$ pint of linseed tea at night. She was to lie much in bed and if she gets up to then lie on the sofa, but by no means to walk until fully recovered. If she felt strong enough to go out and the weather was fine then she must ride in the carriage or be drawn out in a chair. No meat was allowed but light nourishing meals. Milk mixed with water, soda water or brandy and water were advised for drinking. As they were leaving I asked the fee, and it was £10. Dr Evans said that he charged a guinea for every two miles beyond the railway. Charles said afterwards that such is the case again for Fairford having its own railway station, however, it has not, despite much talks and work on procuring it for the town. He then paid Dr Evans, who wrote out a prescription and gave it to Mr Cornwall. He admitted it was a critical case but he has reason to hope that Kate will be restored to health if she will be careful, but an internal complaint like that kind is very difficult to get at or to know exactly what is going on inside. The worst feature is that she has had it for so long. He couldn't but say there is danger in the case and it often breaks out again after it is supposed to be cured and that it often leads to consumption. He examined her lungs and they are perfectly good now, but the bowels and liver both being disordered, irritated one another. It was after 8 o'clock when they left. I was far more excited than dear Kitty was and I spent the interval of their delay in coming in prayer, imploring God to bestow a blessing upon the doctor that he might have wisdom and skill to prescribe that which would conduce to her recovery.

Sun 27th   Mr Cornwall sent his servant with a bottle of white medicine and a blister, but not a syllable with it, he came in the evening and explained how to apply the blister. Alfred Payne called to ask after Kate and spoke of his own father's serious illness through stoppage, he is scarcely likely to live through the night. Mrs Belcher walked over from Arlington and sat with Kate for an hour, then walked back in the pouring rain just after 9. We had no-one to drive the coburg and I dare not leave Kate.

Mon 28th   We have had a sad night. The blister became so intensely painful that dear Kate could bear it no longer. At 3 this morning she called out to me and I lay with her a while, then I woke Elizabeth to go into the garden for plant leaves, but she didn't like it much and didn't offer to hold the candle for me to show her the ones to pluck. She then lit the fire and we boiled water for me to make the cure, she then went off to bed and left me to do it alone. However, it worked well enough and the blister rose pretty well. Frise came over in the evening and staid supper, he talked and laughed too loud, quite forgetting himself and I was obliged to ask him to be more gentle in disturbing Kate. Mr Cornwall called in the evening and is still not sure whether mischief is forming inside but tried to reassure me that Kate will make a fair recovery.

Tues 29th Kate managed to enjoy some knuckle of veal, a little broth and rice. Mr Cornwall came and when he saw that Kate was able to partake of some food, tried to make out that the medicine Dr Evans had prescribed was only the same as he himself had given her a fort night ago, but in different form.

Thurs 31st Kate pretty comfortable. A soaking wet day. I cleaned out the store room with Richard's help. Mrs Hewer sent Kate a rabbit, which I shall cook tomorrow for her. I am very thankful that I do not feel so rebellious, that God does not appear so much in the character of an angry God to me. I do not think nearly so much of this world as I used to do. Ellen Booker called.

JUNE

Fri 1st Kate more comfortable. Aunt B.T. sent her a nice pudding with her kind regards. While I was in the garden I was surprised to see Mrs Howard, she and he were on their way to Faringdon. She was sorry to hear of Kate's illness.

Sat 2nd A pouring rain all day. The parlour grates being painted, had fire in dear mother's bedroom and Kate laid on her bed.

Sun 3rd Frise preached at Meysey Hampton and I went as Charles was able to stay with Kate. Heard from Msr Robineau. He says in his letter that he fears I feel hurt that he did not come here and wishes me to write to him and send a donation.

Mon 4th Mr Cornwall called and saw Kate in bed, then sent another blister. We again had a fire in Ma's bedroom it being so cold and wet. The blister hardly rose, so I dressed it again with plant leaves and when I came in from garden it had risen nicely. Poor Kate shed a few tears. It distresses me to see her so low. I ran over to Frises to ask Harriet to come to sew tomorrow as the linen needs mending. I feel quite poorly and can hardly keep about.

Wed 6th Harriet came to work and Ellen Booker called and looked round the garden. I went to prayer meeting. The Frises thought me looking very sadly.

Thurs 7th Friends are truly kind. Mrs Miller sent Kate a little cooked fish and some jelly, then Mr Lilly sent fish and Mrs Brown brought a small rice pudding. Mrs Frise, always wanting to go one better, sent a Sally Lunn. I assume it was as much to show they had been to Bath as much as present a gift, but had to chastise my quite un-Christian thoughts of it.

Fri 8th Our sheep, being shorn on Wednesday, had to be shut up on account of the very cold weather. One farmer, they say, lost 25 in one night and Archer 12. This is the only day without rain for a long time. Mr Moreton called and walked with me round the garden and orchard. After tea I went to see Mrs Cornwall, she thought it very kind. Harriet staid with Kate. Visited old Abram, saw great change in him but he knew me. His eyes were glassy and he looked as though he was dying. I couldn't help thinking of him all evening. Several times lately I have heard Kate coughing. Had nice letter from Miss Attwater.

Sat 9th Weather still very cold and more rain today. James Cornwall sent a brace of trout this morning with his compliments, and Aunt B.T. another. Mrs Miller sent a glass of jelly.

Sun 10th Mr Manning brought the letters this morning, quite like old times. One was addressed to Mr Thomas, Fairford, but on opening it I found it was for Uncle Ben Thomas from his London doctor. I wonder what ailed him for that, but 'twas but a guinea so could not have been much wrong. I had to send a note of apology as I had broken the seal. Mrs Keyworth wrote to say she was ill. Mr Cornwall, the Frises, Mrs Savory and Mrs Burge all called. Frises supped here. Mrs Thomas Miller brought yet more jelly, but Kate enjoys it.

Tues 12th Another soaking wet night, everyone most out of heart with the continuing wet and extreme cold. We cannot be without fires throughout the house. Charles had letter from Capt Milbourne. He said he is going to Africa soon, but if not, he will come to England at once. Charles found deed of Union amongst the rubbish in bureau. His tongue is quite black, he is quite mawkish, too. Mr Wilson was buried yesterday and old Abram seems a bit better.

Wed 13th A finer day at last. Mrs Frise came in to sit with Kate in the evening while I went to Miss Inman. I chose a Dunstable bonnet and asked her to trim it with white. Uncle B.T. called, so did Ellen Booker.

Thurs 14th   Miss Inman sent Kate a pudding. Mr Cornwall hasn't been again and Kate not so well. It takes the brightness from everything and the only relief from gloom I can find is to think of the time when Jesus will call me home. Posted letters to Alice, Nellie and Lizzie.

Sun 17th   I feel very low about my dear Kate, yet she is so cheerful and has faith that she will be well and strong again, I pray it may be so. The wet and cold has returned. Everything is rising. Mutton is now 9½d a pound and bread has gone up to 6½d. Mr Tovey at the Mill has lost his lambs and so has Mr Iles at the Lunatic Asylum, Tovey's with the rot and Iles's with the cold from shearing. Mrs Wassell wrote of Mr Clarke's death at Clifton, he leaves a wife and 8 children. His sister who was nursing him was called away by the dangerous illness of her sister in lodgings, so they only have a little servant girl to look after them. All is gloomy and grey.

Mon 18th   The first summer's day we've had. A lovely sunny day. I sent to Msr Robineau in French and sent a donation of £3, at least I sent a £5 note to Randall and asked him to forward £3 to Robineau and to hold on to the £2 until I see him again and make up my mind as to the worth of it.

Tues 19th   Back came the cold and wet. Am vexed that Mr Davis has not been over since I returned from London. One of Charles's lambs died suddenly. Our lawn is all under water and Kate was sick as I made her ground rice pudding. Her bowels have not moved yet she took the pill and a draught this morning. Am disgusted that Frise came over to see Kate in the evening when she was feeling a little better, but again has not read to her from the Bible, nor prayed with her. I felt quite hysterical about it all and took refuge in Ma's bedroom, but Harriet was there cleaning up though it was late.

Sun 24th   It is still damp and dismal but a little warmer. Mrs Keyworth staying here is good company and help to me. Mr Yates dined and supped here and folks say he prayed most fervently for us at chapel, though I could not go and tell for myself as Kate is still far from well. In fact I fear for her mentality, she said that if Mr Yates comes to pray with me and talks to me of going to glory I shall be sure to laugh. I fear she is hysterical and think it is her bowels not moving that is causing the trouble so have sent to Mr Cornwall about it.

Tues 26th Mr Cornwall came and ordered an enema for Kate. She got quite hysterical when she saw the soda water bottle being opened so I sent for Mrs Hinks to come and help me give it to her. She couldn't come until 2 o'clock as William was at the critical stage putting the wheel on. Mrs Keyworth left after tea, I was sorry she had to go home. Mrs Savory called but didn't stay. Mrs Vines called and said she would pay me the money as soon as those for whom she had worked paid her.

Wed 27th Thunder and lightening. Poured with rain. Kate's bowels moved and she is quite exhausted. Many evil forebodings as to future prospects. Another rise in prices. Mutton now 10d, bread 7d the quartern and wheat £15 a load. Talk of another comet, even larger than the last. Papers are full of dismal sayings on political matters and the Census Act. We still have fires in the bedrooms it is so cold.

Thurs 28th Note from Keyworths to say that Wassell had arrived in Cirencester and was coming to us, which he did. Spoke to us earnestly on the importance of our making our wills. Charles spoke to me of it earlier this morning and said he felt deeply the necessity of it, but also saw the difficulty of broaching the subject to Kate just now lest she be alarmed by it. It made me feel very sad and I deeply regret not having another likeness of her. Mr Rice called to see her and seeing the Bible open on her bed, picked it up and asked if she would mind a minister of the Anglican faith reading to her. She said she would be pleased to hear it. He did it most nicely, and to think Frise has not even suggested it and he our own minister too.

Fri 29th Went to Cirencester with Mr Wassell as Charles was in all day to watch over Kate. Wassell left on the 4 o'clock train. Emily had slept at Keyworths and dined at the Stephens's. She, the Keyworths and Stephens and Monty came with me to Darby's nursery, then to Gregory's, but being late all the men had left and I could get no flowers. This is the first completely fine day without a spot of rain that we have had for 2 months. Emily said that she had brought fine weather and it augurs well. We reached home at 9½ and pleased Kate was pretty well and comfortable. Harriet had been all day with her and so kind and considerate I thanked God for putting goodness in her heart.

The gateway to the chapel in Dyer Street, Cirencester

❧ JULY ☙

Sun 1st I find it a great comfort having Emily here, she quite cheers me up. I was able to go to Meysey Hampton this afternoon to the service while Emily staid with Kate, then she went over to chapel in the evening. Was vexed to find that Mr Cornwall called while I was out. He told Kate that Dr Evans was coming to see Mrs Beak and could come to see her if she liked. This made poor Kitty feel awkward as evidently Mr Cornwall didn't really want him to, Emily saw through him, and said that as he was leaving he said 'Well, if you wish to see him let me know, he'll be here at 5 tomorrow.'

Mon 2nd We waited in anxious expectation for Dr Evans and a little before 8 o'clock were vexed to see him and Dr Cornwall driving by in the carriage and stop at Miss Tovey's. We could see from the upstairs window where they went. Afterwards Mr Cornwall came alone and seemed a little cross with Dr Evans, said he stayed only 10 minutes in Miss Tovey's house and charged her 2 guineas. It is quite ridiculous to come so late, but we thought his vexation was a sop as he didn't really want Dr Evans to call, thinking he can do for Kate all that is necessary, yet when confronted with his opinion of her he says he still can't speak with certainty on her recovery as there is still some doubt about it. I find it all most distressing and could not even find feeling of any sort at Mr Davis's unexpected arrival, my mind is so full of Kate's illness.

Wed 4th Mrs Miller sent me a note begging assistance. Charles, Kate and I made up a sovereign for her so I took it to her and held on to it as I took her round to the tradesmen to pay some bills with it.

Fri 6th Have been gardening as much of the day as I could spare. Had the mournful news of Col Kingsley's death after one day's illness. Charles and I thought it best not to tell Kate of it. We felt it much how friend after friend departs.

Mon 9th Mr Cornwall called and confided in us that there was a misunderstanding at Cliffords. Clifford had been very insolent to Jim Cornwall. He also said that Lane had taken offence with him over a simple matter and he would not go to his house again, he said he would tell us all about it another time. We gave him a basket of strawberries to take home to Mrs and Susan. He was much pleased. Aunt B.T. called last night in her chair to ask after us. I went out to her and shook hands with her and chatted a while. She was most pleased with the bunch of choice roses I had picked for her and sent last week. Mr Davis arrived. At first he was rather stiff, then gave me a warm shake of the hand. Charles asked him to sleep with him, and he did. He was then soon up to his old tricks, but didn't seem in first rate spirits. He asked to see Kate before he left. We have talked about him much since he left.

Tues 10th Was greatly grieved to hear from Mrs Frise that Mr Legg had just sent a note by boy from Cirencester to say things at Coxwell Street[21] had come to a climax. Mr Stephens has resigned and Mr Frise was begged to supply for them next Sunday. I kept it to myself till evening then told Kate. Mr Frise came over and carried her to sofa in Emily's room. Charles and Emily tead and supped at Frises. We had to put on warm clothing again as the weather has turned cold and cloudy. I gave Mr Frise 10/- today for our sittings at chapel. Emily and Charles did not return from the Frises until 12.

Wed 11th Mr Wassell wrote to Charles to ask him to go to Bristol tomorrow, but Mr Cornwall had asked for our horse and coburg to meet Susan at Cirencester, so he'll go then and I shall go to Cirencester. Kate in great pain again. Charles went to Lechlade to see Locke and made him sign an agreement promising to pay a quarter's rent for Hearman's.

Thurs 12th Rose at 6½ and started for Cirencester at 7 to enable Charles to go by early train to Bristol. I went directly to Mrs Stephens and found her weak and excitable, but enjoying a deep sense of the divine presence of the cause. She spoke of Stephens's resignation as a matter of great humiliation and she begged me not to think the Leggs had been unkind. Said they had done all this purely from the love of God. I envied her Christian spirit. We then went shopping and returned at dinner time when Mr Stephens was home. He seemed as usual and I felt constrained to squeeze his hand. The young people were there so nothing was said. Mrs Stratford called and I walked with her up to the town to Bowly's and was then able to talk on the melancholy subject. I then went to the station and met Susan Cornwall and we tead at Mrs Stephens as Mrs Keyworth had gone to Arlington. We arrived home at 9½. As we passed the third milestone we saw a man behind with a long stick in his hand and a dog trotted before him with a chain hanging loose. Directly after another man was carrying a stout pole. He called the dog angrily to him and they both closed in upon the poor animal and beat him to death. What his offence was I know not, but even sheep worrying could not justify that cruel mode of killing it. Gave £2 to Mrs Stephens for their chapel at Cirencester from Kate and self. Mr Stephens has never asked any of us to give anything.

Fri 13th I was so disgusted at the sight of cruelty last night with that poor dog that I felt quite poorly and could not sleep from thinking of it. Mr Cornwall called and I said to him, 'I hope you find my sister is progressing, sir.' He replied that she seems comfortable but that he would try to see her every day for a while. This gave me the impression that he didn't think so well of her as we do and his words follow me. I was much annoyed this morning when Richard told me our garden was entered yesterday while we were out and two trees stripped of gooseberries. The lovely thrush that built over the summer house door and sat so peacefully, notwithstanding our constant passing in and out, has had its nest robbed and torn down. A prop supporting the old apple tree was pulled up and thrown across the path. I feel so low about the cruelty in this world and I feel rebellious again, though I resort to prayer. I fear God does not always hear me.

Sat 14th   Kate again carried into Emily's room and Mr Cornwall called. Emily and I ran down to see Mrs Burge who is very near her confinement. Greening budded some roses for me and I gave him a shilling for it.

Sun 15th   Kate rather better and with my help walked to dear Ma's room and we had tea there, joined with Uncle B.T. who seemed very gracious so I gave him a pair of Papa's slippers, the oldest ones. His feet were bad, so he was grateful to have them to slip on in chapel. Charles is now at Bradford and seems to enjoy it there.

Mon 16th   Emily busy helping Frises make banners for the children and at 3 o'clock she walked with them to Whelford. Very soon after Eunice and Hannah and Ed Baker drove up. I was extremely annoyed to find that Uncle B.T. had taken Richard and our horse and coburg to Whelford without giving a hint of it, and then kept Richard to help dip the sheep without saying a word, I was greatly inconvenienced by it. Then I saw Mr Frise coaching off, he riding while our visitors walked, it quite mortified me, but by degrees my anger cooled down.

Tues 17th   Mrs Frise brought Kate a pudding, but 'twas very small. Frank and Anna[22] came to tea and ate a lot. Mr Rice came to see Kate and again read to her. I often think he would like to see us attend St Mary's more often, but he respects that as dear Papa was a Baptist minister and follows a long family tradition, so he will not press it, but it is rewarding to know that he is not afraid to recognise us as all Christians together.

Thurs 19th   Heard from Charles this morning. He says he cannot return yet as there is a screw loose at Capt Dyer's. Uncle B.T. called and I spoke to him seriously about the inconvenience caused by him calling away our man and horse and he seemed uncommonly gracious, old rascal that he is. We then made a polite arrangement whereby we would take him to Burdocks, I would then proceed to Furzy Hill and call for him on my return, but a thunderstorm prevented it happening.

Fri 20th   Emily and I went to tea with Susan Cornwall and afterwards called on Uncle and Aunt. She was very poorly but received us kindly enough and was pleased with the strawberries I took. Mr Cornwall called and spoke of Kate going out. I hear it with joy and fear. Oh, guilty mistrust.

Sat 21st   Heard from Mrs King, she says she will come to visit us in our affliction. I do not think she has heard of Mr Stephens's resignation, for she would have mentioned.

Mon 23rd   Went to church to hear Mr Barnes of Faringdon preach. It was a truly solemn and faithful service and the people of St Mary's impressed me with their attentiveness, I often felt during the sermon that our own people at chapel could take a pattern from them in that respect, but then felt vexed at my thoughts, though no doubt the Rev Mr Rice would have been greatly pleased had he been able to read them. Harriet Brown staid with Kate the while as she is making a covering for the sofa and chair.

Thurs 25th   This has been quite a company day. At breakfast time Wakefield came for the property tax. Mr Stephens came after I had been to prayer meeting. He said, 'Well, you know things have come to a crisis in Cirencester. I have sent my resignation in and it has been accepted. We shall leave town as soon as possible, but have to take Ann Eliza to school in London first.' He looked over our new building with a view to taking it for a time, he said much had transpired to make him uncomfortable. He left at 4 and would take nothing but a pipe and a glass of wine. Susan Cornwall called and sat a long time with Kate while I was busy with preserves. In the evening old Parr called, then Mr Hill.

Sat 27th   Mr Parr sent 11 beautiful pot plants, 3 peaches and a bunch of grapes. Kate was delighted and much enjoyed them. Emily and I were early going to prayer meeting and looked at the tombstones. Oh, how my thoughts sunk into the narrow resting place of my beloved parents and how vividly it recalled the past, and how uncertain the future seems. What will be my destiny, what of Kate and Charles, will we marry? The burden of carrying on the household weighs heavily upon me. In the evening a thunderstorm immediately above us intensified my fearful frame of mind. Emily and Kate and I huddled up close together in our bedroom. Kate sent Miss Tovey one of her peaches as there is no hope of her recovery from a tumour. We pray she will enjoy the peach and our faithful wishes.

Sun 29th We couldn't go to Meysey Hampton as Richard asked leave to go home today. Eliza helped me to get Kate into the garden. It was difficult to get the chair through the yard gate. She sat for some time at back parlour door under the verandah and then we drew her round the garden. This is the first time she has been outside the door since May fair and she really enjoyed it, though she was quite unwell in the evening.

AUGUST

Wed 1st Rode to Furzy Hill this afternoon, the first time I have been there since the night before dear Papa's last journey to London. Bessie and Tom had called and staid with Kate. Elizabeth wanted leave to go to tea meeting at Poulton, but I made sure that she set forward to scrub parlour walls so as to put carpet down before Mrs Davis comes. Emily is looking forward to her Ma coming and I wanted to give a good impression.

Thurs 2nd Very busy all day so I didn't have time to meet Mrs Davis at the coach, so Emily waited in the Bull parlour for her Ma to arrive. At first I thought she was rather affected, but it wore off and Emily later told me that her Ma had said that we were just as she had imagined us to be and the very friends she would like Emily to have.

Sat 4th The invalid's better, Kate was drawn out into the garden again. She was poorly yesterday and Mrs Davis quite so, suffering with bad headache. Mr Rice arrived and read to Kate and spoke very nice to us, we thanked him kindly and he said he would come again in a fortnight before he went to see his father. Went to Meysey Hampton, me riding the pony and Mrs Davis and Emily in the coburg, we visited the schoolroom and they wrote in visitors' book.

Sun 5th Mrs Davis delighted with our little chapel and rooms. Saw Richard's mother at Hannah Vincent's when I called and felt compelled to have serious words with her.

Mon 6th It was wet all morning but we had sent to say we would go to Arlington and could not get out of it. Mrs Davis enjoyed the views and seeing school. Mrs Davis joked me much about the possibility of me becoming also a Mrs Davis, Emily had spoken to her about Mr D and I was glad he was not there, but felt disappointed that he was not at Belchers either, for he must have known we would call on them.

Then, he came to tea when Mr Belcher returned, after which we had music. Mr D sang and played, then asked if I would take him back to Fairford and give him a bed. After we had supped he joined us and we all enjoyed ourselves very much when we got home. Kate had a nice fire in Emily's bedroom and we all went there and had hot elderwine. Harriet had gone home.

Tues 7th Being fine we all went to the Park House gardens. In the first hothouse we met Mr Thomson and William and they showed us all round, they came back with us for tea. Kate so much better that she came down and for the first time since her illness sang a duet with me. Heard that Mrs Hanks has died.

Wed 8th Very wet and cold. Mrs Davis, Emily, Mr D and I went to see the lovely stained glass windows at St Mary's. The Rev Mr Rice and Mrs Joyce[23], servant and child were there, a sweet little fellow. They were pleased to see us. Mrs Davis and Emily then went to Frises and Mr D and I had time alone in back parlour. He was full of fun as he has been every day. Last night we asked him to shut the shutters in the store room, intending when he was in there to lock the door, but Mrs Davis and I couldn't quite manage it and he jumped out. We had shouts of laughter, 'twas such fun.

Thurs 9th Emily and I went to Cirencester to see her Ma off on the train. Mr D had to go early, he asked if he should look for someone at Lavington as he was going home for a week or two. I looked up at him and said, 'Yes, by all means, and I hope you will be directed to a good one.' He then looked sad and we parted coolly for we were behind time and had to drive straight to the station. Mrs Davis said she liked Mr Davis very much and they kept up the joke of calling each other mother and son. Emily and I then went to Keyworths and started for home at 7. My heart was heavy as I thought I should see nothing more of Mr D – oh, dear John, I find for the first time that I rather liked you. My, what a surprise I had on our return to find him still there. He appeared sad, anxious to leave, but more anxious to stay. I gave him a kind release, some bread and cheese and rice and a great stick. Lighter of heart he set off at 10 o'clock. Mrs Hanks's death hurrying him off. Charles returned from Bath last night unexpectedly and seemed much better for the change, but says he must go to Ashford tomorrow. He was out with Uncle B.T. so saw little of him.

Sat 11th Went to see old Abram. Poor man, he's very grateful for all we do for him and says he shouldn't have lived so long without our kindness. He thanked me for the wine and I told him not to be afraid to drink comfortably for there should be more for as long as he lives. I must say I wonder daily at how he rallies round each time I think the end is near. But I feel I must do something to show Our Lord my gratitude for his over-ruling the troubles which caused a dark cloud to hang over us lately and threatened to drive us from our home.

Sun 12th   Went to chapel but my thoughts kept wandering and thinking about Mr D. Determined to concentrate more, I went with Emily to Meysey Hampton in the afternoon but found Mr Smith's service very cold, so it did nothing to alleviate my perplexity on the matter.

Tues 14th   A fine, warm day. As Kate seemed so bright I had Richard draw her through the town down to East End to visit the Cornwalls. Everyone who saw her was pleased as it is many months since she has

The Cornwall's house, Court Close

been in the street. Mrs Cornwall was quite overcome to see us and the old gent gave Kate a hearty welcome. Susan had gone to Lechlade. They made us take a glass of wine and Mrs Cornwall and Charles both gathered us a beautiful nosegay each. We met Mrs Moreton on the way to dine at the Rev Mr Rice's, but she was quite put about having lost her belt and buckles.

Thurs 16th   Dull and damp again. Susan Cornwall tead here and Evelyn came with her. I was disgusted with him. He is very ill-bred. He said Fairford is the dullest hole he was ever in in his life, he was quite tired of it. He seemed to forget the kindness of his grandparents in giving him a home when his parents lost theirs. Nothing was good enough for him. I went to see Mrs Burge. She was confined. Lotty went with us to Arlington tea-meeting yesterday. I sent to ask Uncle B.T. to join us, but was sorry he accepted, but thought it only right to ask him. I was excited to see Mr Davis again, but he kept running about busying himself as though he did not know what to do for the best. I went with the Keyworths and Mr R Belcher to see the spring in Bibury. We then returned to the Belchers for supper and Mr Davis joined us. We had a little music afterwards and dear J kept my brooch. He said he would come over on Monday. I felt I had some liking for him still and my heart was sufficiently drawn out to him as to allow me to catch his eye once or twice, a thing I rarely or never do.

Fri 17th   I wrote to Mr D to ask him to take care of my brooch and to bring it with him. I seem to long to see him, yet feel I cannot quite accept his advances. Emily seems to like him and hopes I shall not hastily put him aside.

Sat 18th   So cold we are obliged to light fires again. I began with Emily to make wax flowers and she and I made a jasmine spray. Had Nanny to dine here. We had a letter returned from Australia, it was written by dear Papa to William and John, dated January 10th 1859, only three months before his death. It is singular to have brothers so far away in distance and apart from us.

Mon 20th   I was as busy and as brisk as a bee all the morning expecting Mr Davis. Then, as Emily was rolling my hair, we heard him playing the piano. She put me on a velvet bow for the first time and Mr D said it made me look younger. I have worn it rolled twice before and didn't like it, but today everybody did. I felt I had an increasing liking for Mr D and found he has for me, and yet my judgment is against it.

He tried hard to make me say 'Yes'. I trembled at the thought of it, and could say nothing I wanted to, though we had much time alone. I confess it perplexes me much. In the evening we enjoyed making music together. We were much amused when he asked for a night-shirt, having forgotten to pack his. I gave him one of my gay night-gowns, which he wore.

Tues 21st   Mr Davis made us laugh by saying that he could scarcely sleep for admiring himself in his fine nightgown. This day has passed much as yesterday. I know not what to do or what to say and cannot say what I wish. He said he cared much for me but the difference in our position had sometimes made him think it was quite useless to pursue his wishes. Emily went to chapel, and Kate, Mr D and I sang and played music. He detained me when Emily and Kate went in to sup and Kate seemed annoyed by it when we went in. He again detained me against my will when they had retired for the night.

Wed 22nd   A pouring wet day so we were surprised to see the Keyworths coach up. We had cut our leg of mutton in two, but we made the most of it and they left at 7½. Mr Davis left after dinner as he had friends visiting him for tea, he said he would write. I told him not to think too much of me but to go to God for direction. I told him I could not get J.W. out of my mind, though I had so long tried to and I mistrust myself about him. He said he could not see that as a valid reason for objecting, and as to Kate he thought her health was improving all the while. He said he should like her to come and live with us if that would help me in accepting him. I told him I would pray for guidance in the matter. He then wished Kate goodbye in bed, and asked her to take care of me, to see that I walk in the garden every day and go to bed early. I got Richard to drive him to Arlington it being so wet. Mr Keyworth and his wife seem very fond of each other I noticed, but she's a coarse woman.

Thurs 23rd   Mr Frise and I started for Cirencester at 10½, riding nearly to Norcot then sent the horse back. Being fine, began mowing barley today. Went to the Stephens's as we hear they would be leaving Thursday. Poor Mrs Stephens looks the picture of despair, she says her husband talks of the painful subject but little, and if she mentions it he is silent. Miss Mountain gave Sarah Mary lesson in music and staid supper. Poor Morty feels it much and looks sadly. He was most grieved to hear Mr Legg say at chapel that he hopes God will show Mr Stephens what havoc he has made of his people and give him true repentence. In the afternoon we walked to Dr Vöelkers, she had just returned from a drive after her confinement with first girl, they were very pleased to see us. Staid night with the Stephens.

Fri 24th Mercy. Not a bit of sleep have I had. Directly I laid down in bed I was tormented with company. I felt all over drawers, shelf and table to try and find matches to light the candle, but in vain, so sat up in bed in patient distress waiting for the first gleam of daylight. Oh, what a night it was. I felt as though I was being eaten alive, when it got a little light I caught two large bed bugs just going home to their hiding places. Mr Frise had staid the night with the Keyworths, oh, lucky him, but the Stephens have much trouble just now and I could not mention my distressful night between their sheets. They go to Deal on Thursday. It is strange how Mrs Stephens will not hear a word against the Leggs, but their spirit appears to be very vindictive. Kate seemed quite comfortable when I got home, Emily had been most attentive to her.

Mon 27th Kate very poorly again. Dear Charles returned this evening and we were very glad to see him. Uncle B.T. went in our coburg and brought him back from Cirencester. Some of the church at Coxwell Street are determined to invite Mr Stephens to continue amongst them for a few months longer, it will be decided at church meeting tomorrow. Mr Parr sent Kate some grapes and nectarines. Emily and I called on Mrs White this morning. She was most gracious and picked us some currants. Was intrigued to hear from Charles that the Captain is engaged to an Independent missionary's daughter. He would now only stay in England a week or ten days. This must have come from Randall's brother, who is in Jamaica. The news seemed to give me relief, and also Kate, but we've had much fun over it. Emily seemed much disappointed as she likes Capt Milbourne, but then she likes Mr Davis, too. Lotty Coles came to tea and Sam came to supper.

Tues 28th I felt quite a trial talking to Charles about Mr Davis, but I told him all now that the news has reached us of Captain's betrothal. Charles said he could say nothing against the Rev John Davis, in fact he rather likes him and was quite satisfied as to his being a man of piety, for that is the primary thing. He thinks he would be kind and he could therefore give me up to him more comfortably than to many others. He said, 'if you think of it you must at once have your property settled on you.' However, I feel everything is very uncertain and I am very fearful of such motives influencing me as would not be honourable to God. I also have thoughts that Mr D is not *quite* good enough for me and that I might do better.

Wed 29th   Our flower show! I set to work and with Emily and Richard gathered some fine pears and gooseberries and arranged them in the round tray in dishes, two of pears and two of gooseberries and fringed them round with willow and made a pretty nosegay for the centre. But, alas, by the time I had finished it it was too late for the competition, but we sent the cases of minerals. Emily, Charles and I went down at 2 and for some time the company was very small but afterwards increased. Mrs Joyce spoke to me in a very friendly manner as did Mrs Moreton and others. Mrs Coles told me much about Mr Stephens that made my heart ache and I began to think worse of matters than I had previously. Had a letter from Keyworths this afternoon to say that the church meeting resolved to re-elect Mr Stephens. I invited Mrs Cook and Bessie Coles just to tea, so was annoyed to find Bessie and Gregory Faulkes waiting here also and staid tea. They were at the show but I had not intended that they should be included as Boswell Belcher and Mrs had come as well. The show was much better than the ungenial season led one to expect it would be. The vegetables were particularly fine.

Fri 31st   Kate a little better. In the afternoon I went out into the garden to sketch our house and in the evening Kate and I sang duets together.

⚓ SEPTEMBER ⚓

Sat 1st   We have a couple of lovely sunny days. Just as we were out in the garden and I sat down to my sketching the drawing room doors opened, and lo and behold, Mr Kidd made his appearance much to my surprise, not having heard anything of him for a long, long time. He looks thin and pale. We met Kate halfway up in the orchard, Susan Cornwall was drawing her along in the chair. Later, Charles took Kidd to Burdocks as he had brought his gun and wanted to go shooting. Had a letter from Mr Davis this morning. Thank goodness, it was a sensible one. I do not feel very warmly towards him today.

Mon 3rd   Mr Kidd drew Kate round the garden in the chair then placed it in warm corner by the summer house. He sat on the lower part of it and made me sit on his knee whiie he told us of his courtship with Agnes. He says he is sure he shan't marry her now, though he has furnished his house beautifully. He doesn't seem in first-rate spirits.

Tues 4th Kidd went out to try and shoot partridges for Kate. He came home saturated with dew and was obliged to change his socks and trousers, then had to dry them before leaving on the coach. We miss him already but he talks of coming again soon and says he would like to bring his brother as he is anxious that we should meet. He says he is very pious and would just do for me.

Fri 7th I wrote to Mr Davis and read it first to Emily, she thought it a very respectful letter. I did not invite him to come round here from London, though he asked if he should. My affections are not increasing towards him, but I am still awaiting the will of Providence about it. I do desire that no sinful or unworthy motive may be allowed to actuate me either way.

Sat 8th Poor Abram died at 1 this morning. I saw him Thursday and thought him going fast, the last thing he ate was an egg which I sent him. Heard from the Keyworths that Mr Stephens has declined the re-election to the church in Cirencester. Emily and I went to the Crofts Chapel to hear Mr Handel Cossom. He was very solemn and correct.

Mon 10th Mr Cornwall called to see Kate. He brought the tidings that Mr Beak died today and Mrs West died on Thursday. Mr Davis was rather expected to return by coach, but didn't arrive. Emily and I went to Dorcas meeting at Mrs Nicholas's and when all were assembled, by some mistake, there was no wine so I had to run down to the Market Place and purchase some from John Wane.

Tues 11th Just as I sat down to wax flowers, Mr Keyworth came so we all went to Burdocks as he was able to draw Kate in the chair. Charles said he would stay in case Mr Davis came, but he did not. I felt quite disappointed, but would not admit to it, neither did he write.

Wed 12th The morning being very fine, we walked to Quenington. The Bedwells arrived soon after our return and spent the day. As I let someone out of the door, Emily called out, 'Oh, Sarah, here he is coming.' Sure enough it was Mr D, but I maintained a coolness to him all evening. He begged a bed for the night as Mr Keyworth was staying, too, and they both pleaded bad headaches and a feeling of being unwell, he staid.

Thurs 13th   Emily took Kate out in the afternoon and Mr Davis took me up in the summerhouse and staid till tea-time. He brought me a brooch and Kate a locket. I felt sad and perplexed when he gave me the brooch as I knew not what to do about accepting it, but he said that he had received so much kindness from us that he wished to offer it as a little present. This put it in a rather less objectionable light, but then he insisted on pinning it on me and, to my mind, took a rather longer than necessary time in the doing of it.

Fri 14th   Charles took John Davis to Burdocks this afternoon and after tea John and I went up in summerhouse. I had hard work to make him go to chapel as he felt too full of fun. However, I made him go and Emily and I followed. He supped at Frises.

Sat 15th   I was very busy all morning and Mr D went up to the study till dinner time. In afternoon, Emily again took Kate out and John and I staid home. I am in a straight, not quite liking to give him up and yet feeling I can't settle to accept him. I have asked the Lord what to do and He does not answer me. The thought that I might do better in this life is no honour to God and is not, I fear, a good motive. Besides, I quite like the fellow, but I do not feel he is so eminent for piety as I could wish and would be no help to me in this respect. I was annoyed this afternoon when Charles brought Mr Cornwall through the garden into front parlour where Mr D and I were sitting on the sofa. When I let Mr Cornwall out, after seeing Kate, he said rather pointedly, 'I am so sorry to have disturbed you both.' It quite mortified me. Mr D left at 7, leaving his portmanteau to be sent back at the tea-meeting. His last words were urging me to take care of my health, to drink the bark that Emily gives me, and to walk out every fine morning. He told me that he loves me and I must love him in return. To this I was silent. I said he should get married and not wait for me, so he asked me when I should be ready. I felt happier after he left.

Sun 16th   I went to take Mrs Frise's class, but managed to spend the time getting the children to sing, much to my relief.

Mon 17th   Charles has 4 acres of barley out still, and again it was a pouring wet day.

Tues 18th   Last evening we received three papers from Jamaica, dated 15, 17th and 18th August and one from New York, all in Capt

Milbourne's handwriting. Mr Cornwall thinks Kate going on well and advises if the weather clears to go to the seaside.

Thurs 20th Went down to tell Mr Cornwall that Kate not so well again. Susan asked me to cut her bird's claws, which I did for her. Miss Tovey is taken with trouble with her bowels, too, but Mr Cornwall says that he does not think there is mischief afoot with Kate's. We all had letters from William and John. It grieves us to see that they are raising money on their property, being in financial difficulties. We feel we should help our brothers, but are unable to do so at this time.

Fri 21st Was surprised to hear from Elizabeth that she is thinking of leaving us at Michaelmas, but she did say that she was still considering it and nothing was definite. I had to ask the Lord to take this over, as he has never left us completely without a servant before, but He has my problem over Mr D to sort out first. Mr Cornwall called and told us about a boy that was shot and said his bottom was like a plum pudding, and when Charles came in he said 'Well, Mr Kingsley, it is the old man tonight and not the young one,' referring to last Saturday. Collett brought me a parcel from Cricklade. Kate seemed quite excited when he drew up the carrier's cart, I believe she thought it might be a visitor. It was a little present from Ann Laight. She sent five little bunches of carnations, each tied neatly with a flower and underneath were two pairs of beautifully worked sleeves. I showed them all to Mr Cornwall and it quite affected him. He said it showed a feeling of great respect. Their servant left them last Saturday in a very disrespectful manner. Kate and I are so overcome by the poor girl's kindness, but do not know how to acknowledge it as she cannot read or write. This afternoon also had a letter from Capt Milbourne, dated September 20th 'At sea off Wales', addressed to Charles asking when and where he could meet him, begging a line by return. Charles addressed a letter to him at Post Office and invited him to Fairford. Poor dear Charles was much worried by a letter from Wyldes. He was expecting a balance of £200 and had only £36 odd.

Sun 23rd Cold and frosty. Autumn tints are very general. The beech tree is already really yellow and our walnut tree strews the ground. Often the trees are not so bare in November as now. I feel so dissatisfied with myself and mourn my shortcomings. I feel my heart is very hard sometimes. Very few at Meysey Hampton chapel, called at Mrs Hewer's and left some peaches.

Mon 24th   Mr Cornwall called. He joked me about 'changing my state'. I told him I didn't think I should do so, and he said that if I did he hoped it would be for my happiness.

Tues 25th   Frise came in and smoked a pipe. I arranged with Elizabeth to stay another year. Mrs Hinks was called out from chapel to see to Mrs Parr who is being confined. As Harriet is away, Mrs Frise said she would stay with Kate while Emily and I were out.

Thurs 27th   Started at 8 for Bourton. Emily and I took Mrs Cornwall as they are without a horse, the doctor needing it for his visits. We put her out at Clapton and we drove on to Kendall's. The bride was too gaily dressed and to my mind didn't look very bridal. Richard Hall and Miss Hall called. I felt excited and think he did too somewhat. Mr Kendall junior was very chatty. They live in Foster's old house and have everything beautiful. Bessie Chalmers I didn't much like. After lunch we went to see Mr Beddome's study. Mrs Brooks was very busy house-cleaning and at first demurred to our going up, but everything was in beautiful order. On our return from seeing the chapel we went to see Mr Burnet's children, I was much pleased with them. After dinner Richard Hall seemed to lose some of his restraint. I felt excited again when Agnes joked to me about him. We left after a cup of coffee at 7. As we left and driving over the bridge, which is quite unprotected by even the slightest rail, the horse shied and turned short round and ran back. The wheels of the coburg ran back off the bridge and just escaped going over into the water, had it done so I fear there would have been loss of life. The horse sank on to its knees twice and much alarmed us. We picked Mrs Cornwall up at Clapton turning but said nothing to her of our fright. It rained all the way home, but we were thankful it was in safety, though we rode in fear.

Sat 29th   Busy washing all day yesterday, Emily quite poorly, the Howards came to tea but didn't stay long. This morning Capt Milbourne wrote to Charles saying he will be here today and leaves for Africa on the 12th ultimo. I went with Richard driving to Cirencester and arrived at 3 o'clock at Keyworths. Found Capt Milbourne there. I suddenly felt very glad to see him and thought he looked better than ever, and secretly admired him. After we had tea, we reached home at 7. Capt seemed delighted to be here once more and his prayers and thanksgiving were most affectionate. Having heard he was engaged, I appointed Charles to find out the truth of it.

The Baptist Chapel, Meysey Hampton

Sun 30th Capt Milbourne went to Meysey Hampton and spoke to the people there from the pulpit, they were all most attentive. He took as his text, 'Please remember me' and I felt his eye wander in my direction. He took my hand on returning from chapel. In the evening we had music and he chose to sing hymns, in which Kate and I both joined, I couldn't help comparing his choice with that of Mr D's, for a minister, I fear Mr D often overlooks hymns for more popular tunes.

OCTOBER

Mon 1st This has been an eventful day for me. Going hastily into the front parlour, not knowing Capt was there, he was very affectionate. He drew me to him and said, 'Do you know, Sarah, that tittle tattle is very busy about you in London. They say you've committed the unpardonable sin of giving yourself to another – the Rev Mr John Davis of Arlington. It's not true, I hope, for I've been foolish enough to think of the same thing myself.' I was dumbfounded and could say nothing, except that I had come to no decision about it and had given Mr D no answer as I seek the hand of Providence in the matter. He urged me no further. After breakfast Mrs Frise ran across to see him.

Capt wished Charles and me to travel to Dublin to see him off, but we could not, but did take him to Cirencester station, taking Emily with us. He took an affectionate leave of me and said he would write from Newcastle. We had taken sandwiches to eat in the park but when we called on Mrs Keyworth she insisted we dined there. Mrs R Belcher and Bessie Coles came in much to my annoyance as they are now sure to relate same to Mr D. He was supposed to have come today and my heart is anxious to know what his reaction will be when he hears the Capt has visited. On my return I told Kate what had transpired and it made her very low, for she fears my leaving her for a husband's following. It cast a shadow on my excitement as Capt told me that his wife on her dying bed wished him to have Alice East and had written to Mr East. Her father, the Rev William Knibb[24] is highly regarded in Jamaica and is regarded as one of the leading figures in the emancipation of the slaves there. Mr East was uncertain of the advisability of the match, and Capt told me that he had written to Mr East and said it was out of the question on account of her youth, so he was released from that now. He said Alice is far too young, on account of his having a small daughter to bring to a marriage, but what he also said was that he had thought of no one beside me. It seemed singular that everyone should speak so highly of the Captain. Mr and Mrs Frise admired him very much and even Elizabeth can't help talking about him to Kate. Emily much admires him also.

Tues 2nd I feel a little annoyed with John that he neither came nor wrote. I helped Mrs Frise decorate the chapel for the tea-meeting and Kate sent over a note to say that he had come, but I played it coolly and did not come home until 3. We were rather cool with each other at first and he took Emily to chapel and I called for Mrs Frise, but she had already gone, so I entered alone and found him sitting with Emily and she had all the talk. I could not help my thoughts and eye wandering from Mr Arthur's preaching, which I termed heavy and tedious, to where he, dear J was sitting. He staid the night but I ensured I was not left alone with him.

Wed 3rd Mrs Savory and Mrs Snelling and 2 children called this afternoon. While we were in the garden, Mrs Savory told Kate that she hears Mr Davis and I are to be married. This afternoon I received a very long and loving epistle from the Capt, and he seems to take it for granted that I accepted him on Monday, adding how pleased his sister Mary is, she too wishes me to go to Dublin to see him off as he will be at sea some months. It distracted me quite a lot and I am in a tearful fix as I did not think I had given the Capt the least ground for his thinking so, I feel it most dishonourable to dear J and I couldn't bear the thought of that. I was quite upset the rest of the day and it makes me cling to dear John the more so.

Thurs 4th Lotty Coles came to ask Emily and I down to tea and dear J said he would come down for us. Kate went for a ride in the coburg for the first time and bore it pretty well, though she couldn't bear a trot. Charles and John were in first rate form at supper time and we had much fun as the Burges came too and wanted to know which of us three John comes after, Kate, Emily or me. So he took more notice of Emily then in fun, but a little too much for my liking. Then when we were upstairs Mrs Burge made me cross by saying that someone said to her 'What a pity 'tis Miss Thomas doesn't do her courting in the house and not in the garden.' She told me to set me on my guard. She said she thought it was said to her in a nasty manner but wouldn't name the author of it, but said that who ever it was had seen dear J kiss me. Emily suggests it is our common enemy Uncle B.T. Mrs Burge sadly wants to know who Mr Davis is after.

Fri 5th　My spirits deeply depressed. I pray for guidance and God doesn't seem to hear. I am in great perplexity as I have always cast my troubles upon Him who is supposed to hear all people. I question myself as to my spiritual worthiness and get more depressed as I count my shortcomings. I had some conversation with John this afternoon and he presses me to give him a final yes, but the more he presses the more I hesitate. I love him much and am assured of his affection for me, I can't say Yes, but I dread to say No. This evening I wrote to Capt to say that he had misunderstood my position and told him I couldn't enter into any other engagement till I had given my final answer to Mr Davis. Charles received a letter from Capt sending a note of introduction for us to meet Mr Hope in Liverpool as there is a blemish in the ship and that could delay his sailing.

Sat 6th　The worry and anxiety wear me out. Mr Davis now says that he can't go home to Arlington tomorrow and preach if I say No. I promised to think it over and urged him to pray over it. He said that if I turn him away he will go to Kate for he loves her dearly, too. I told him I should like that, but my heart aches over it for she has been suffering much in her bowels again and I fear she would not stand up to marriage. I gave dear J a basket of damsons and gave him a warm farewell as I saw him off through the green door. I pray it was out of sight of prying eyes this time.

Mon 8th　Elizabeth went home today for a holiday and Nanny came to do for us. The Dorcas meeting was held here tonight. Had to put another blister on poor Kate after Mr Cornwall had called.

Wed 10th　Sam Burge came with us to Sheephouse, but 'twas a wet day. He started on about Mr Davis, then said 'Well, we say he is not quite the man for you'. I fear this might influence me, so I changed the subject. Mrs Burge staid at Sheephouse and it was almost 1 in the morning when we arrived home. Elizabeth hadn't returned but Harriet was sitting up for us. I heard a little noise as I went to sit on the sofa and lo and behold Mr Davis popped out from behind it. I was both glad and sorry for I had consoled myself that he would be prevented by the heavy rain in coming, although he was not invited to Sheephouse. I tried to be cool but was struck to see how ill he looked. His face and hands deathly cold. He said after the others had retired that he was so miserable he couldn't stay at Arlington. He says it will kill him if I say No.

Sat 13th　Dear John still here. It harasses me much. I like him more and more I am with him, he sets every obstacle I name on one side. He is so affectionate and watches my every move. Had a letter from Capt, saying he was surprised at my letter to him but trusts all will be well. He says he had told his friends at Newcastle that he was coming home in the Spring to be married. Mr Davis wouldn't take dinner with us, but said he would walk home with a bundle of bread and cheese, which he did though 'twas pouring with rain. Later it cleared up and I went to see Mrs Alex Iles and was much struck with her consumptive appearance, she has been ordered to Torquay for the winter. I tead with Miss Iles at Park Corner school, the young ladies very quietly at their studies.

Sun 14th　The wet continues, but Charles, Emily and I went to Cirencester to hear Mr Stephens's farewell sermon. The chapel was crowded and we could see all the opposite party there. He said he had nothing to bring as a charge against anyone and didn't appear before them either as a defendant or complainant, simply as a minister. He supped with us after at Keyworths and Charles asked him to preach at Meysey Hampton next Sunday. I was most put out when I was introduced to Mr Stolker on coming out of the chapel as I said we had met before, at Bath when I was with Mr Wassell. He said he thought I was Mr Wassell's servant. I was mortified and blame all the worry I have to bear. He tried to apologise but I haughtily dismissed it.

Tues 16th　Made some elder wine today. Feel a little more trustful. I seem to think more of John that I do Capt, but thoughts of both will intrude, did a little sketching in the garden.

Fri 19th   Mr Cornwall called but was sent for to see Simpson at Kempsford. The pony ran away and threw him and boy out, but they are not much hurt. I went to Dances and put the Dorcas books right. Had another long letter from Capt. He has not had mine and still talks of 'bringing matters to a head in the Spring, when I shall call you mine'. He says he earnestly sought God's help in the way his affections should be directed and his desires remain with me. I am in perplexity on it, for God answers me not in such a manner. John also intimated the same, so I feel very awkwardly placed as I do not want to offend my Heavenly Father. Capt says he will not expect me to go to Africa or to leave dear Charles and Kate, now this is something I don't like. If he cannot get a home for me I might as well keep as I am. He proposes going backwards and forwards to Africa and England, and I couldn't bear that either.

Mon 22   Was grieved to see that Morty Stephens took beer repeatedly with his pipe at supper last night when Mr Stephens came to preach at Meysey Hampton. Even Emily trembled for him, Kate seemed to also, but I fear it was more on account of the enema I had to give her earlier. I tead at Frises and gave Anna a thorough scolding as I thought her quite tiresome.

Tues 23rd   Hewitt, Mr Davis, Mr Brooks and Mrs Frise came to Arlington with me in our coburg and King's horse. Mr Hewitt, in speaking of Capt said he was a lovely Christian man, but could never do any good for himself in a wordly sense as he is only fit to drive a ship. I could see dear J took all of this in, and I felt it weigh heavily on my mind that Hewitt should say so much against him, so I gave him up in my own mind as his is such an unsettled life it would not do for me.

Wed 24th   Called on the Frises and converse turned on to dear J. I told them it was me and not Kate that he came to see and they were surprised. They advised me not to let him stay so long at our house, said folks at Arlington would be dissatisfied and he ought to be careful as a young minister. They said also that he was not the one for me. They had heard also about the gossip of my courting in the garden, said the party talking about it lives in Fairford, but it isn't Uncle B. Thomas, neither is it Harriet. I have felt all dark and gloomy all day over it as I cannot fix to have either dear John or Captain Milbourne. Yet I dread being all abroad again as it would be nice to be settled. The Frises like the Capt, but say it would be an anxious life for me.

Fri 26th   Charles and I had long talk over the Capt this morning. Charles seems quite sorry that I have told him I have written to decline his offer. I scarcely know how to disentangle myself from dear J and I think that is what decided me.

Sat 27th   My way seems quite hedged up. I fear my motives in declining Capt are not altogether worthy, yet I fear a hinderance to giving myself away to John Davis, for many still say he is not good enough for me. It makes me sad to think of giving them both up and living an old maid. Charles has received a letter from Capt asking him to intervene. We had a little fun yesterday drawing lots[25] to decide which I should have, dear J or the Capt. Charles, Kate, Emily and I all drew the Captain. Poor Charles has been sadly worried last few days. He had long and rather heated conversation with Uncle B.T. and is evidently fearful that B.T. may give us all much trouble. Charles says he is determined not to give up the land, and twill be at a great loss.

Tues 30th   Mrs Frise told Emily that Mr Humphries could speak of nothing but Kate when he tead there after Mr Davis had brought him to Fairford last week. He confided in Frise that he wished he had her for his wife, but after making enquiries here and at Arlington thought he would not have enough money to be of our family. Mrs Frise said that she spoke so highly of Kate as she wanted to make Humphries jealous, but was not pleased when he said he would look to a servant girl instead as he had no property of his own to offer a wife. She said she thought I should have the Captain and John should marry Kate. I racked black grape wine off this morning and Mr Cornwall called as I was busy. I asked him if he thought Kate's health would justify her thinking of marriage, as there was a gent in question. He seemed surprised and said he could not speak positively. Mr Robb and his Kate drove up at 6½ and wanted to sleep here. He would be going by coach to London tomorrow from the Bull and his Kate would return to Ozleworth. She begged me not to say anything about the baby to her Papa before she did. Emily and I went after they had left to take apples to the children at Meysey Hampton school. I then went to Sarah Short's. Took a warm red dress of dear Ma's to Ann Truman and a black jacket and trousers for Vincent. When I returned went with Kate to Mrs Hinks to ask about the wheel William is repairing for us and bought an armchair from Calebs. It was his mother's and we paid him 10/- for it. Rodway brought the horses and dog cart and Kate rode in the latter down to the East End to visit the Cornwalls.

The Village Green at Meysey Hampton

❧NOVEMBER❦

Thurs 1st   Called at lunatic asylum and thanked Mrs Iles for the loan of the chair as Kate now feels she is strong enough for walking again. I fear sometimes she seems too well.

Fri 2nd   Very busy stopping down wine and sorting apples. Sent half a sack to Mrs Cornwall and made an apple and damson pudding for her supper as Mr Keyworth and Smith came to sup. I felt quite over-done, and hardly fit enough to travel tomorrow.

Sat 3rd   Dear Emily quite poorly but would come with me to Wotton Bassett. Called at Cricklade and took Ann Laight some apples and pears, she was delighted. Jessie met me at Weymouth but I felt very sadly with violent headache. All welcomed me warmly and Mrs Davis and Mary got me a chop. After supper I spread the hamper on the floor and they were delighted with the leaves that dear Kitty had gathered yesterday and with the fruit from our orchard. They shouted with gladness.

Mon 5th   Have felt quite poorly since being here. All very kind. Mrs Davis made me hot port wine and water which revived my spirits. Mary, Jessie and I went to lecture on dissolving views in chapel and Sir J Franklin's expedition, then we walked on esplanade and enjoyed the views very much.

Wed 7th   Mrs Davis gave drawing lessons in back parlour and Mary and I dozed in front of fire. Heard from dear Kate and Emily, they are as usual. Had music in the evening. Mr and Mrs Birt called, I thought Mrs was a little affected in her manner.

Fri 9th   Still bitterly cold. Dreamt I had a long letter from Capt from Madeira but I woke before I read it. Mamselle Raymond came to tea, a stout person but possessing some good sense.

Sat 10th   Heard from Charles and Kate. She informed me that John is very friendly with her, I seem to hope that he may take to her, but no doubt I should feel it for some time if he did.

Sun 11th   Felt sorry to see leaning towards churchism in Mr Birt who came to dinner after his preaching at chapel this morning, and almost so in Mrs Davis. I was quite shocked to think of it. Had a nice letter from dear J, but I didn't open it for a long time.

Tues 13th   Mary went to Bridport. Mrs Davis, Jess and I went to Mace's and I ordered a seal skin cloak and bought a magenta palisse, then we walked to the Nothe. The expanse of sea view reminded me of our waiting for Everetta at the Isle of Wight and brought Captain Milbourne very much to mind. Went to Miss Tizards to tea and felt unwell when I got home, but after some hot rum and water felt better.

Wed 14th   Weather milder. Mary, Jessie and I went to Birts for tea and Mrs Davis came after. They would make me dance a highland fling at which Mrs Birt roared with laughter. We had music all evening and I quite enjoyed it all, then Mr Birt walked home with us. Poor Mrs Davis is so upset by Lewis lodging and boarding at Birt's and did not make his appearance. She talked to me about it in her room until after midnight.

Sat 17th Wrote to Mr East in reply to his letter of a week or so ago. Wore my new cloak to call on Mrs Benson. Wrote to Kate and John, enclosed in hers. Told him I couldn't see matter in any different light. I have thought about him so much these last few days and it made my heart ache to write so. I feel I must now settle down to old maidenism.

Wed 21st Still unwell, Mrs Davis's doctor made me up a draught and only today have I kept any food down. Had arrowroot for lunch and potatoes and gravy for dinner. Read Dickens's 'House to Let'. I dreamt that Mary Beddome placed a bible before me and said 'Here, look, Tom wished to call your attention to this', and her finger pointed to the words, 'Fear not, for I will be with thee'. It is a pleasant dream to think of, that Capt should convey a message in this way of his thoughts.

Fri 23rd Mr Edwards came at 3 o'clock and stopped teeth for Mary and Jessie and two for me, charged me 1/-. He put gutta perch in another and charged nothing. A lovely day, Mary and I went to Mace to pay for my new seal skin cloak which cost £1 16s. 6d. Mr Benson called to offer to take us to a lecture on Circulation of the Blood. Had letter from my dear Kate, she is not so well. She did not get the letter I posted from here on Saturday night until Monday afternoon. She said John was anxiously expecting one from me and seized it immediately and afterwards he was miserable and walked round the garden though it was dark. Then he went out with Charles and didn't return until after 11 o'clock. He asked her to read the letter and she thought it cool. Went to Birts for tea and Mrs Birt took me into Mr Lewis's room as he was out, but I fancy he came home after tea and she sent him off. There's something very strange about it altogether. They said they could not ask Beddonies there as they could wish because the ladies could not receive the least attention from gents without misunderstanding what was meant. Mr B said they were very deceitful appeared one thing to Mrs Birt and another to him. I felt shocked by what I heard of the Lewis affair, and they thinking everyone thought so highly of them.

Mon 26th Very wet, stayed in and wrote letters and worked on my velvet jacket. Heard from Mrs Wassell. She wants me to go to Bath. Also had long letter from Kidd, he wishes me to go to London to see him. Wrote to both to decline.

Tues 27th A fine day. Mary and I went to the museum and saw the caste of paddle of Plyosauris found in Portland Bay, the original is at Dorchester. I was delighted with the sea anemones. After dinner went with Mary first to Birts to invite them on Friday, and Lewis went out when we got there. We then went to visit the Stranges. Mr Strange said some very strong things about Mary's hat. I was glad of it as she thinks everybody admires her in it. Mrs Davis worries dreadfully about the Birts and the Lewis affair, and cries about it. I really am quite sick of it.

Fri 30th Heard from Kate. Her liver is disturbed again. She told me they had found out that it was Mrs Rose, the tailor's wife close by, who saw dear John kiss me in the garden. Mrs Rose told Leas the tailor in London Street in front of Lotty and Emily Coles. I wish I was home. We played old maid in the evening and that did nothing to lift my spirits.

DECEMBER

Mon 3rd Went to Birts to dine, Lewis was said to be out. They made me sing all afternoon. I had to struggle against vanity as they said so much about liking my singing. They said they enjoyed my visit. I was shocked to hear from Mrs Birt that Mary said someone in Fairford is very fond of Emily. She admitted that someone was Charles. I had no notion of it. She told me also that Mary had told her that I had had two offers and there were always several gents at our house. I was most vexed at this tittle tattle and knew not what to do. Met Mr Lewis on the bridge on way home.

Tues 4th Had long talk with Mary about conceit. I think she tries to see how far she can go into the world and yet be Christian. She thinks me too rigid and strict. I do not enjoy her society and when she plays she is very rough and boisterous. I told her that if Christianity dwelt in our hearts we think little of concerts and the like, because our pleasure should be in more heavenly things. After tea the Birts visited again and insisted I should sing to them and praised me much. They paid me many compliments and I could see Mary did not enjoy them doing so.

Thurs 6th Mrs Davis in bed with headache. Jessie and I went to chapel early. I gave 5/- to Mr Birt as I felt I had profited from his preaching, and I gave 6d to the blind lad. Jessie and I sat at Mrs Birt's table, Mary's I noticed was filled up with boys. Mr Lewis went upstairs and only spoke to the girls as he left. He then shook hands with us all. Mrs Lundie had her mantle stolen out of her pew.

Fri 7th Mr Birt called to bring me a time table and told us that when Mrs Birt had passed Mrs Tizard's, two men caught hold of her, one tried to seize her pocket and the other her watch. She screamed and someone opened a window and started screaming and the men ran off. I left at 12 and a stout man got into the omnibus. He was very anxious to continue with me and as I thought he was elderly and a Quaker from his conversation I agreed he could ride in the same box, thinking I was favoured. When he got out at Yeovil he took my hand and then tried to kiss me, and as soon as the other passengers got out he came back in to renew the insult, but happily others started to come in and demanded him to make way for them as he was stout and filled up the doorway. I was never so insulted before. I reached Bath soon after 4 and Sarah Wassell met me. It was very wet.

Sat 8th My birthday. No letter. I wrote to Mrs Davis to thank her for my stay. Felt dull all day shut up alone with only Sarah for company as the Wassells shut themselves up in the other room. I felt in the way.

Sun 9th Heard Mr Mitchell from Canada, a mulatto, preach in the morning, though 'twas more of a talk. Tead at J Bedwell's and much enjoyed their converse. 'Twas good to be there.

Wed 12th Heard from Kate this morning, she is not in good spirits. I have dreamt of her three nights in succession and thought I was displeased with her about something. She has not seen dear J since he had my letter. Sarah came with me to see Dr Highmoris and I told him all of Kate's symptoms. He said he feared she had organic disease of the liver, which nearly overcame me. The consultation was three-quarters of an hour and he charged me £3 17s. 6d. Mrs Tom Attwater is at point of death after confinement, she was worse this morning and then felt better this evening and ate two oysters. She then wanted her bed moved, which I fear is a very bad sign. We left her at 8 o'clock.

Thurs 13th Weather is fine but cold. I was busy at work till evening. I hear the thrush singing beautifully every morning before I am up. I don't feel very comfortable here. The Wassells sit much alone in the study and Sarah and I in other room, and we don't have much kindred feeling. She is not very considerate, she takes me long walks even after I complain of pains in back.

Fri 14th   I called on the McMichaels, saw Mrs and Annie. The Wassells then came with me to the Archard's. They are a most interesting family and I for one appreciated the bountiful tea and supper. We had cutlets and forcemeat balls, a most handsome joint of cold beef, potatoes whole and mashed, hot plum pudding, mincepies, jam tarts, beside some others, and a beautiful salad. Sarah and I sang duets and also Emma. I liked her least of all. We returned at 11½. The best day I have had since I've been here.

Sun 16th   Heard from Kate again. I had long talk with Mr Wassell about John and Capt. He thinks Capt acted very prematurely and thinks it doesn't show good judgment. Mrs Wassell won't hear of my having the Capt. She says John is much more suitable, being a minister. They also cheered me by saying that they are sure Kate will be well again and, one day, married. I feel the Wassells give sound advice and despite their shortcomings in hospitality I truly believe they have my interests at heart. Mr Wassell spoke again after we had supped on the subject. He is quite averse to my having Capt unless I can take him to my home and provide for him if he hasn't enough to retire on. He says if Capt continues at sea I couldn't bear the knocking about of going on a ship for long periods, and if I staid home I should soon die of anxiety for him. I feel the truth of this and perhaps this is the hand of Providence I have prayed to direct me. I had just put all thoughts of Capt from my mind when William Hill came to say goodbye to Sarah. He leaves for Australia, and she has done nothing but cry about it. Silly girl. I shall be so glad to get home.

Wed 19th   Heard from Charles this morning wondering where I am, so wrote to him immediately to say I'd be in town tonight by 9 and asked him to meet me. It started to snow thickly, but I didn't regret my decision to leave. I packed my luggage after breakfast and Mr Wassell promised to send it on to Fairford. Mrs lent me a small carpet bag to put my nightdress in. John Firman helped me put cover on my box as Sarah was still in bed. Left station, getting third class, and reached London at 9. So pleased to see Charles at station to meet me. We went together to Walducks.

Thurs 20th   Charles and I went with W Thurston to finish some business and left him to pay into Masterman's the sum of £1. We dined opposite the Mission House and returned to Walducks for tea at 9.

Fri 21st   A busy day. Snow falling thickly. Randall called and he took me to Gower Street as he had business nearby, so I called on the Murphys. All pleased to see me. The horse omnibuses all full and the ground so slippery, Charles missed his footing on the step and mercifully escaped being run over by the wheels just in time. Kidd had called at Walducks while we were out so came again at 9. He was uncommonly free and said he would like to come for Christmas, but I didn't pursue it as I am hoping that John might come.

Sat 22nd   After eventful journey with horses slipping with the omnibuses, we managed to catch the train on time and was so thankful to see Richard at Cirencester with the coburg to meet us. A young woman in the train at Swindon told us that one of the porters was carrying her trunk across the line at Maidenhead and the train took him and tore his clothes to pieces as he was getting on to the platform and his leg was torn open. Delighted to see my dear Kitty again, and Emily says she will stay for Christmas.

Mon 24th   While busy making mincepies, Mr Davis walked into kitchen and was as usual. Kate in fun tried to make him think I hadn't come home and he looked dismal over it, but soon changed when he brought his wet boots into kitchen and saw me there.

Christmas Day.   It is very cold and frosty. The rime frost as thick as snow and presented a most exquisite appearance. Emily and I went into garden to see the trees. The elms in the orchard were lovely beyond description. The dark branches looked most rich with their foliage of snow-like feathers. Charles and dear John walked to Meysey Hampton in the afternoon and in the evening we had music and different games. It has been a merrier Christmas than we've had for years.

Wed 26th   Mr Frise came over to wish Emily goodbye as she leaves tomorrow. Mrs Frise came after and I was shocked to hear that she had heard at Whelford that Milligan left his wife and children and went to Canada and died. They lived a wretched life.

Fri 28th   The snow still beautiful, but sharp frosts make it very cold. The kitchen all frozen up this morning. John again urged me to consent to his proposal. He says he loves me more and more. He said he loves every eighth of an inch of me three times over. We have had much fun with him and Charles this week. Emily gave Charles a good tickling on the floor twice, then John came into my bedroom before he left. I was so vexed that Emily came and found him there. She said she wanted to say goodbye and couldn't find us. She spoiled it completely for us as I felt quite inclined to give way, but on reflection think it might have been providential. Richard drove John as far as Coln and then he walked to Arlington. Mrs Box wrote this morning begging help for her son John. He has failed and has been in London for 3 months waiting for a situation and is now going to one in Manchester. He needs help to pay for his lodgings and for clothes and his fare to go to Manchester. I wonder at her doing so.

Sun 30th Yesterday went to Cirencester and glad of warm wine at Keyworths. Heard from them much that is dishonourable about Mrs Box and it shut my heart for the present until John has been obliged to help himself. Paid £250 into Charles's account, transferred from our own, then withdrew £50 for our own expenses. After such sharp frosts the weather has turned to torrential rain making travelling very dangerous. The wet has come into our study like a flood and through the ceiling into bedroom.

1861

❦ JANUARY ❦

Tues 1st Last night Charles went to watch at 11 o'clock for the changing year. I had called at Nanny's, then took flannel shirt to Francis's wife and one to Paish's. Received note of hand from Charles for £500 from our account. Had but little sleep from ramping toothache and feel middling today. Mr Cornwall made but a nominal visit. Poor old man, he looked quite poorly.

Thurs 3rd Had the Frises over for tea and had a romp with them in the hall. Master Frank drank three glasses of home made wine. Went to see Harrison and Polly Woodman.

Sat 5th Richard gave notice this morning. He said he wished to leave in a fortnight and knows he has not been giving satisfaction lately. He intends apprenticing himself at Halls in the trade of carpenter but as he will still be at Milton End he will come to our aid when necessary which I considered very good of him. Charles, Kate and I tead at Frises. They did all they could to make us comfortable, but oh, the dirty little drabs of children. They were out sliding till 5½ then when they came in sat on the hearth rug to have their tea. Jesse sopped his toast in his mug of tea then put in his dirty little paw, took it out and squeezed it dry, then poked it into his mouth. I could scarcely go on with my tea, it was so disgusting to see the dirt running down between his fingers and into his cup again. They are not managed at all and there was no peace until they were all in bed. Mrs Frise made Kate a little cornflour pudding and we supped round the fire. It was cold when we left and Mrs Frise wrapped a big shawl over Kate's head and I carried her bonnet. Mr Frise gave her his arm to cross the road as Charles had left earlier to write. But he was out when we returned and didn't come back until ½ past midnight, having been with sadler Burge down the Market Place.

Mon 7th   Yesterday was the first day set aside universally for special united prayer. Went to prayer meeting tonight conducted by the Rev Mr Rice of St Mary's in the Crofts Hall. The Methodists as usual made much noise. Bought some warm petticoats for some old women at Meysey Hampton.

Wed 9th   Bessie Booker called and so did Sarah Short, gave her warm wine and bread and meat and a petticoat. Packed up mincepies and bacon for her to take to her aunt.

Fri 11th   Went to Cirencester as Mrs Tranter told me of gardener, but I couldn't stay to see him. We had a good warm at Richard's and a glass of grog, then went to Keyworths to tea.

Sun 13th   This has been a bad sad day for me. Everything has gone wrong. Mr Davis does not come or write and I shall put him out of my mind as such worry hinders everything. There was extravagant talk at breakfast time which annoyed me, then I broke a bottle of rum and oil all over my dress and carpet. Elizabeth was very contrary and kept us waiting a long time for everything at dinner. I had to scold her thoroughly. Then Kate heard her talking to Richard and said she wished it was her last Sunday here. I went to see poor Mrs Bedwell, she was very wandering and watched Martha so narrowly round the bed I fancied she wanted to speak to me alone. Gave warm petticoats to Hannah Vincent, though she be an old cat, Betty Miller and Martha Ecott. Snowed fast all evening.

Mon 14th   It is the deepest snow we've had. Charles had to go to Cirencester on business with the bank, so he got Charles King from the George Inn to take him. Just as Kate and I had dined and removed the cloth a gentle tap at the parlour door made us jump. In walked dear J, thoroughly tired and his feet wet. I felt reproached that he should have walked from Arlington in the deep snow for my answer, for that is what he said he had come for. He said he was tired of suspense and if I didn't accept him he would go to Emily B. He said he wouldn't have much difficulty in obtaining her. He said she gave him quite a hint the other day. I was most vexed. I felt he looked dejected and didn't have the heart to say what I normally say to him that he must wait until I receive guidance.

Wed 16th   My romp with dear J appears to have cheered him up. I gave him some hot wine then, in fun, I sketched him and Kate together with their arms round each other. He left at 4 and said he might come again in a month. I was sad when he left and had to resort to prayer as I'm so afraid of my own evil heart. Had to pull myself together as Mr Smith arrived and tead here, he came for his payment for preaching and I paid him £13 up to Christmas 1860. Then I felt annoyed with him as he is so determined to give children tea now, so Kate and I decided they shan't have books too. We wish they had books rather than tea, but he has already promised it to them. Kate cut open Spurgeon's almanack today.

Fri 18th Errands of mercy all day. Took a Dorcas shift to poor Jonathan Cowly's wife and found him alone, so took the opportunity of urging him to repent for his sins. Took worsted stockings to Thomas Simpson, a child's shift to Mabbets and a pinafore for Shurmer's child. All were grateful.

Sun 20th Very mild, snow all gone. Had lovely letter from John, he wants us to go to Arlington instead of us going to Stratford's lecture.

Tues 22nd This has been a lovely sunny day. Richard cut his head open with grubbing axe getting up parsnips as the frost is not out of the ground. I doctored it with Hatfield's tincture.

Thurs 24th Charles went to Cirencester bank and Creese paid him the money to go to his cousins, £1,700. Heard with sadness of poor Mrs Bedwell's death. I shall miss her. Have finished reading 'Heir of Redclyffe' but it does me no good. The death of Guy makes me sad and I feel the influence is not for my betterment. It is seldom I read a book of this kind and I hope I have the strength to make it the last for a long time as I feel my reading time is short and would be more profitable to my spiritual understanding if I kept to religious works.

Sat 26th A most lovely day. Called on Susan Cornwall. Mrs C said she has recently heard several times that I am to be married to a Baptist minister and he lives at Arlington. But she said she denies all knowledge of it to the parties and says 'Miss Thomas would never let herself down like that.' I could not say what I would have liked to and my mind was much hurt to hear dear J spoken of like that, although I realise he is not good enough for me and I can do better, but I am very fond of him and cannot give him up lightly. Mrs Rice sent her missionary basket for us to see and we purchased a large pincushion for 5/- to help the Church of St Mary's overseas mission.

Mon 28th   Kate walked in the garden as it was so fine. She went to chapel yesterday and all seemed pleased to see her, smiling and nodding kind congratulations to her from their pews. It is a long time since she has managed to attend there. At 12½ dear J came and the day passed much as usual but we had a strange occurrence at night. All had gone to bed and Elizabeth was asleep in the back room. Kate and I were undressing in our room by the light of a cheerful fire and suddenly were startled by the apparition of a figure in white. We both stopped, rooted to the spot, neither of us spoke and then it vanished as suddenly, and we both remarked upon it.

Tues 29th   We decided we would not mention the apparition to anyone, we did not want the servants upset and I fear Charles and John would have had sport over it. I cannot help notice that John seems very attentive to my dear Kitty. I sometimes wish they would unite and at other times I am afraid of it. I think many would judge him harshly if known that he had already proposed to one sister then turned to the other. I cannot bear to think that I would be left with no one to love me though, and I have not made up my mind about Capt Milbourne for when John is around I am attracted to him for motives which I fear would not be approved upon by God, but such are my inclinations and I have to resort to prayer to steady my desires. It makes me quite poorly and dear J too, I think. Though I believe that our present malady may be that we dined off Jim Cornwall's old hare. Late afternoon John and I started for Arlington, Richard driving. We tead at Belchers and when dear J had gone to take his singing lessons Mrs Belcher said, 'Well, we shall soon have you to live here, shan't we.' She was surprised when I said there was no engagement and she begged me make up my mind and settle soon. John came to supper and came part way home, then walked back.

❧ FEBRUARY ☙

Fri 1st   Richard whitewashed the store room yesterday and I have been busy all day. Mrs Rose washed the things. The dining room was crammed full, Mrs Rose and Elizabeth were scouring up to their knees in dirt when lo and behold Mr Tovey and Mr Savory arrived and said the boys Sam and Bob would be here presently. The only room free was the kitchen and I had to get Elizabeth to sweep it up a bit for them to go in there while we set to and helped put the things back in the store room. They all stayed and supped, then smoked until 1 o'clock in the morning having drunk a quart bottle of gin, *full*. I was

The Square, Bibury

dead beat, Kate had to retire early and even Charles was glad 'twas over.

Sun 3rd Had letter from Emily she is anxious to know if I had given dear J my answer. Had letter from J saying that he could have diagrams on Livingstone's Discoveries in Africa for lecture, as Charles wished it. Charles walked to the school[26] at Meysey Hampton for the first time, but he would only put three Abernetty's in his pocket.

Tues 5th George Clissold wrote and asked for bed for tonight and at 2½ he and Annie arrived. It put us about no end having a big wash about. Kate and I had to alter the beds as Elizabeth was busy baking cakes for the children's treat, then Mr Smith and Mr Rolt came and staid tea.

Wed 6th A stormy day. Richard came from Hall's soon after 3 and drove us to Meysey Hampton. Kate and I have been busying ourselves looking over our old clothes and doing them up in bundles and ticketing them to give away in the village, we also took some wine for the poor people. Charles and I had fine fun carrying milk in a huge jug and tin can. All enjoyed the tea enormously and looked uncommonly happy. Sarah Short and I cut up, Charles, Smith and Page waited on them. Afterwards we went to prayer meeting. I was surprised Richard addressed the meeting, then G Clark, but all he could say was to object to evening services beginning at $6\frac{1}{2}$.

Sat 9th   Charles bought fruit trees in Cirencester, travelling by carriers cart to get them in. Frise came over to smoke and brought news that Mr Stephens is very ill in London, he has been taken insensible and that Lord Gifford broke a blood vessel. Charles received a letter from Mr Davis asking him to get Collett to take diagrams by his carriers cart and says that although he intended to come on Monday it will not be until Tuesday. I felt it deeply and could not refrain from tears. I know he thought my last letter cool and I feel this is the beginning of his turning away. Kate felt it too and thinks we shall soon lose sight of him altogether. Charles said that his not coming until Tuesday would cause confusion, so he wrote and asked him to try and come on Monday as planned. This *is his doing, not mine.*

Mon 11th   Frosty with snow storms. Charles opened the green door for dear J and I set out little dog to face the road to warn us if he was coming. Kate and I sat alone all afternoon looking for him but he didn't come.

Tues 12th   I went to Brown's for a chop for Kate and on my return found John in the back parlour. He shook hands with me very coolly and seemed distant. He paid me little attention, but much to Kate. I felt quite poorly but made an effort to go to the lecture. Charles helped him put up diagrams and the chapel was crowded when I got there, our seat and all. Mr Davis gave a most interesting talk on Dr Livingstone's travels in Africa and everyone listened to the lecture most attentively. Many said how they enjoyed it. Some of the people said to me that he was such a nice young man he made them love him whether or not. I felt the truth of it. When we got home I was quite overcome and had a sad attack of fainting, but it was dear Kitty who helped me crawl upstairs. Mr Davis only stood at bedroom door to say goodnight, yet he could see how weak I was from the vapours.

Wed 13th   Mr Davis asked Kate to sew a button on his shirt sleeve, though I was standing by. She refused and he asked me, so I said 'No'. He then went out saying he was off to the Market Place and would come back to Frises. It was dinner time when he returned, but it was alright, he had been to Perrott's for a haircut and shave and could not have been long at Frises. He made a fidget with his sleeve and Kate said to him when I was out of the room that she thought he had been unkind to ask her about the button in front of me. Later he asked me if I would sew it on for him and then detained me in front parlour and asked me to forgive him. He said he was sorry to have caused me pain, but his mind had also been pained as when he left here last he had to go to Winson and Mrs W Coles said to him that she had tangible proof he had been rejected, and he felt the hurt of it. He thought it must have been something I said on my last visit to Arlington. He began to feel that he must now make a difference and come here on a different footing. He said he should never understand why I could not accept him and he would now go to Emily Beddome at once, if I could recommend her. I said I thought she might be more suited to him, though I was wounded to say it. I brushed his hair and his coat for him before he left and we parted excellent friends and I said we would always be pleased to see him and would always reserve a bed for him. He said he believed I had acted from conscience and not my heart. He thought it would be honourable to return our letters. I told him he should have his but not to trouble to return mine. He had engaged to tea with several others so we had to scurry about to find a horse, ours being out. John Poole was using his for his baker's round and King at the George was using his, then mercifully, B.T. returned ours in time and Charles drove him to Bibury, but it was snowing quite thickly by that time.

Fri 15th Kate and I chatted over matters. She would like me to have Mr Davis for she likes him a lot. He has intimated several times he will go to her if I reject him, so I wonder at his saying he will go to Emily Beddome. I suspect it is because he would not be able to face coming here for Kate and seeing me after we have been so much to each other. I fear I could not stand it either, but know not what to do. Kate and I kissed and tried to make up our differences over it.

Sat 16th We were amazingly shocked and grieved to hear today that Mr Stephens is said by the doctors to be going insane. Oh, sad, sad smoking!! Mortimer walked over this afternoon, he feels his father's infliction so deeply and Mrs S is very sadly. Having passed through so much ourselves we have heartfelt sympathy. We gave Morty a bed for the night we could not bear to think of him walking back to Cirencester after supper in such bad weather. He was quite wet through when he arrived and his boots not dried out.

Tues 19th Susan Cornwall came to tea, she was quite agreeable and better company than Annie Clissold proved to be. She arrived by afternoon coach yesterday and isn't gay company. She says nothing more than Yes and No when spoken to. I took her to see the lambs at Burdocks. Charles went to Cricklade with Uncle B.T. and sold cow and calf for £16. We called on Aunt, she was quite gracious for a change. Said she would return the call and come down garden to see Kate, but had heard she was worse. What nonsense. She is better now than for ages.

Wed 20th   A boisterous day. Charles started for London by coach. He had been summoned to do so by Whitchurch, asking him if he was satisfied with Wyldes and urging strictest secrecy. Charles wrote to Kidd and asked him to meet him in town, we feel deeply anxious about it. Francis drove us to Meysey Hampton, I took port wine jelly to Bessie Hewer and some books.

Thurs 21st   We have had the most terrific of windy nights I ever recollect. It kept us from sleep and frightened us sadly. I thought the house would fall down. I looked out several times at Brown's house as the roof is off for re-roofing. This morning the Browns had much difficulty in getting tarpaulin fastened over roof it blew so hard. Richard was so worried as he had much upholstery work stored there. Reports circulated round the town when the waggon arrived 12 hours late, of the road being blocked by an empty house which had blown down. Everybody's shutters were blown about and at Newent 79 trees on one farm alone were blown down. Everyone was in fear of losing their house around their ears.

Mon 25th   After much trouble got Francis to drive Annie Clissold and self to Cirencester. She left by train and we are not sorry to part with her. Heard from Charles, and Kate heard from Kidd, to whom Charles has given the management of the affairs. Whitehead met them at Grays and implied there has been foul play at Wyldes, but thinks Charles won't hurt if he's careful. He says he'll see him alright and paid to the full. We're in care about Ottoman Shares as they talk of closing the bank entirely and returning money to the shareholders. Elizabeth was most impertinent and when scolded went into Nanny. She has been forbidden to go without speaking to us of her movements. I was all for her going at once, but thought I had better commit the affair to God before I can take any step.

Tues 26th   Yesterday when I called on Mrs Stratford I was quite took to finding John there. He was just leaving but sat down again. I scarcely know what I said and when I left he did. As we walked towards our carriage I was taken by such a nervous attack of shivering I could scarcely step and had to cling to his arm. He was quite alarmed. I said that it was the wine I had at the Sparks's, which was true enough, though I did have some wedding cake with it so 'twas not on an empty stomach, but I didn't tell John that. He said he should ride home with me as I appeared quite faint and I did not demur. I quite forgot that I had promised to give Mrs Moreton a ride back to Fairford and we had to return from Norcot for her, she was most grateful. I soon recovered and when we got home John was quite natural with me again, and quite warm. *We had fun upstairs.*

Wed 27th John and I breakfasted alone, and afterwards showed much warmth of feeling. He again tried to talk over matters and I shed tears freely. After dinner I let him out of the green door and watched him out of sight from the summerhouse. I do not understand myself. I love him dearly and I think I could never love anyone so much again, and yet I seem not able to say Yes to his proposal. I fear that I must accept the hinderance is with me for if I do not trust in God to direct me I shall become an infidel. I must accept that He is faithful to His promises and He will answer in His own time – though it be long in coming.

Thurs 28th A lovely day. Herbert came to cut the vines. Called on Mrs Rice to borrow 'Mrs Winslow' for Ellen Booker. Merrick Holme came in and looked so ill I thought it was he and not Mr Lane, who was also there, who must be suffering from disease of the heart. I fear Mr Holme is the blind leading the blind as far as Christianity is concerned. The steel medicine which Kate is taking seems to be doing her good. Martha Brown looks like a corpse and has dreadful cough. She had a job to sit up in bed when I called and between her bad bouts of coughing she told me that Mrs Mills, from the *other chapel*, had told her last Wednesday that she is sure to die and would probably go to hell. She said she had worried about it ever since and had not been able to enjoy anything. When her mother went downstairs, though timid about it, I prayed with her.

❧ MARCH ☙

Fri 1st Last night we rang bell and had Elizabeth in to talk to her about her conduct. After tea I visited Ann Wall and Nancy Green, found Mr Frise smoking pipe here on my return. Then Mrs Frise came over and when Kate and I were talking of how we considered Widow Payne was harsh with her child John, Mrs Frise fired up, saying she should have done the same thing. Then she added, 'And you've enough temper in you to do it, I can just see you sweeping the child out of the door in a fret.' She was evidently vexed that she had said it, and she could see we were both annoyed and shocked at her remark about me. She was sorry she spoke so hastily and hoped we would forget it. Had queer note from Jeffery again, wanting to spend time here. I wrote to put him off altogether as he said his expenses to and from Swindon must be met by Mr Smith. Poor Miss Tovey died. She gone and dear Kate spared, though both with the same complaint. When I was doing hams in the kitchen with Elizabeth I broached the subject again of her conduct if she stays here. She said she will only stay if I give her her Sundays as she doesn't like going to chapel, especially to Meysey Hampton. I was vexed and shocked and told her that we must part if those were the conditions as I would not agree to them. Frise hung on until late and as usual asked for pipe before we rose from table. He again tried to set aside family worship for the pipe. Oh, evil pipe.

Fri 8th Mr Wassell has been here since Tuesday, he and Charles have left again today. Jeffery wrote again. He must have consummate impudence to do it. I see clearly what he wants, *a wife with tin*. I am very glad Mr Wassell has warned me against having Jeffery here, and I have now put him off entirely. Sent a sperib with Charles for Mrs Keyworth.

Tues 12th We miss Charles sadly. On Sunday went to Meysey Hampton and took more port wine jelly to Mrs Hewer. Miss Silvester and two little Hobbs's called. The Dorcas meeting was held here, but only Mrs Nicholas, J Iles, Mrs Reynolds and S Vines came. As I have not been at all well, Mr Cornwall came again this morning and asked me many questions about myself very particularly and was most kind. Have heard from Charles and pray everything will be sorted out, it is fortunate that Mr Wassell spares the time to be with him. Uncle B.T. came in after tea and asked Kate Howard, who is staying here, to sing to him, then he lectured her for being so over careful of her voice as not to sing out. Still have no gardener and no servant in view. Kate Howard and I went to Ebenezer chapel last evening and heard Mr Hazelrick, most solemn, so I suppose, profitable.

Thurs 14th A lovely day. The two Kates helped me do some

gardening. Was most grieved to find that an egg had been taken out of nest in manger in orchard. Elizabeth found Francis in store on Sunday feeding fowls and the gates locked, though he entered through them. I feel sad that suspicion should fall on Francis. B.T. called again this evening. He tries to find out who dear J comes to see. I was shocked that he should say that Miss Beddome was far too ladylike to fall for Mr Davis, as 'I consider him a coarse man.' Kate leapt to his defence before I could find my voice, and B.T. said, 'Ah, I see which way the cat runs.'

Mon 18th Kate Howard left this morning, Mr Dance put his horse in our coburg and drove her. I felt very awkward as she wished me to go too, but this is the day dear J said he would come. I wanted to go badly, but didn't want to miss him. What makes it so vexatious is that he didn't come. I opened the green door for him and foolish me, I watched in the summer house for him for a long time. Mrs Belcher and George Malins came to dine. George walked round the town while Mrs B, Kate and I talked of Mr Davis. Mrs Belcher is very fond of him and wishes I would accept him. As they left early, and I was feeling so mawkish about Mr D not coming, I took little Anna Frise with me and we walked with them to the top of the second hill. My good kind brother met us on the top of Coln hill to walk back with us, bringing cloaks as it had started to rain heavily. He had brought pigeons from Kidd on his return.

Tues 19th My mind still agitated, Mr Cornwall called again, he said that Bessie Hewer died on Saturday. He told me he had heard of a servant at Cirencester and of Ann Arkell. Had letter to say that Alice and Ellen East are on their way to England.[27]

Wed 20th I ran into parlour before breakfast and found three letters for me. One in large writing that seemed familiar, so I opened it hastily and found that it was John's. He apologised for not coming on Monday, saying he was going out. I read it hastily, devouring his every word and my eye rested on – 'I shall not be coming again as the week following I shall be marrying.' It so upset me I could not read another word as my eyes were filled with tears which flowed so readily. I ran upstairs and threw the letter on Kate's bed and she could hardly console me. I could not hear her words for some time as I was racked with uncontrolled sobbing. Then, dear Kitty, put her arms round me and was laughing as she pointed out that he was marrying a couple the following week and the wedding would delay him for a while. It took me the rest of the day to accept his odd idea of fun, and we both felt vexed with him for trifling with my feelings, especially as he had addressed me as Miss Thomas, the first time he has ever done so. By night I felt quite weaned from him. Then our canary died without warning. I shall carry out the post mortem tomorrow.

Thurs 21st   Kate and I very busy cleaning out study, Susan Cornwall called. I opened up our poor canary after she had left, and found that its gizard was out of place.

Sat 23rd   Charles helped us to garden as we are still without a gardener. A young woman came from Quenington to offer as servant. We sent for James Westbury as we heard that he is offering, but on seeing him he wanted 12/- a week and beer. I don't like him much.

Wed 27th   Charles very kind running about trying to get horse to go to Cirencester, he drove me. Saw Emma Parsons at Miss Weights, and after much bopeep work, I discovered she is a member of Primitive Church, but I liked her and agreed with her for £8. My mind was on the fact that John was supposed to come today, the day I had to be in town to fix for servant. Susan Cornwall was staying with Kate and would stay tea so Charles and I supped at Keyworths then staid to see Gyngells fireworks display. William Flux got out of gig and came to speak with us. Saw also Morty Stephens and Miss Mountain.

Good Friday   Thought much of this day 12 month. No J today and he didn't come on Wednesday. I wrote to him this evening a very cool note asking him to let me have the names and numbers of the books he borrowed from our library as Kate and I are busy with books and doing the study. Wrote to Lizzie East and visited Martha Brown. Sad to hear the news of death of Humphries's child. Martha asked me for black crepe to make her mourning bonnet. B.T. came and read his lecture paper, which though I admit to not understanding fully, appeared quite good. I cast many anxious looks across the green but still no sign of dear J. My feelings were both vexed and disappointed.

APRIL

Wed 3rd   Walked to Mrs Hewer's to tea as Mrs Wells and children were to be there also. Billy Dunn cleaned all our windows after I had cleaned out museum in morning. Charles and Uncle B.T. went to

Marston Meysey in coburg, then on to Cirencester for Charles to pass overseer's account.

Thurs 4th Mrs Keyworth came to dine, couldn't come earlier as Orlando had measles, she told Kate that Mr Davis was home and had been to Sheephouse with Coles and slept there, but he had been very poorly so I suppose that explains why he didn't come. Drew first rhubarb for Mrs Keyworth to take home.

Fri 5th Harriet at work yesterday and today. Had short letter from dear J to say he had badly swollen and gathered face. I called at Cornwalls but Susan was at Bath. I took Mr C a bottle of French brandy and expected to be asked to tea but Mrs C seemed busy. Gave Elizabeth a holiday today.

Mon 8th Elizabeth bustled with her work to do all she could before she left at 10. She shed many tears before going. I got Mrs Wall to come at 2 to clean up as Elizabeth had left all corners filthy and the dough trough in a disgusting state. I am not sorry she has left now. We all set to to clean through properly before Emma Parsons came at 7 as I want her to see the standard I shall expect of her. Poor girl, her brother-in-law died last night.

Wed 10th Fear Emma is a little bit of a muddler, but seems willing to learn. She told us to our surprise that Elizabeth had had a child in Cirencester and it is with her mother. On this news I gave Emma a book called 'Truth made Simple' and impressed upon her the value of truth in all things and spoke most plainly to her. Charles took deeds of land at Burdocks to Cirencester yesterday and brought back deeds of Hannington Farm. Charles and I both had a letter from Captain Milbourne this morning. This is first since he sailed. He talks of coming to England this year. There's a large ship lying anchor without Master and he expects to bring her to Liverpool. He still has his favourite idea of remaining in Africa. In mine he says though he 'is rejected' I shall always esteem you as a dear friend and Christian sister and trust the past will not be allowed to interfere with a friendly correspondence. We were pleased to hear from him again.

Thurs 11th Harriet came to work again and much annoyed me by saying 'I want to know about Mr Davis presently,' then added, 'I hear he goes to see a lady in Bibury', but wouldn't name the party and I did not want her to see I was interested, so did not press her.

Sat 13th Mr Cornwall called and said he heard I was to be married to Mr Davis, and again I told him No. As yet I like Emma very well, she seems very willing to learn, but isn't very particular in dusting the room. I had to call her in after breakfast and point it out to her and she thanked me. This evening wrote out copy of my Will, to be signed before I go out.

Sun 14th Heard from Mr East this morning to say Alice and Ellen sailed on March 6th and would reach England during last week of April or first of May. It was a kind letter, more like former days. Had letter from Kidd begging Charles and I to go to Grays at once and stay there.

Mon 15th While I was gardening John walked in through green door. He looked quite ill and we both felt restrained. We went indoors and I gave him glass of port wine and he seemed affected by it, and made me have some and then we began to feel at home again. At bedtime he carried the warming pan for my bed as before. I was really glad to see him once more.

Old Arlington Chapel 1747-1833

Tues 16th   Heard from E Beddome and she wishes me to send her a servant, so I got Francis to drive and took dear J to Arlington. We walked to Ann Arkell's and hope she may do to go. Went to Belchers and staid supper then John came part way home with me, and walked back.

Wed 17th   Mr Cornwall called and paid Kate and I several pretty compliments. Went to see Aunt and Uncle and the sick folks before Charles and I started for town. Found Randall's house full, had to sleep with Sarah Wassell in tiny bed in back parlour, we could scarcely turn round in the room.

Fri 19th   Went to Mission House this morning with large group. Miss Waskett visited and we chatted about Jeffery. Everyone said he much admired me when he saw me here in 1857 and said he would look after me were he not engaged to Miss Waskett.

Tues 23rd   Had busy few days, many here and Charles and I have visited many old friends. On Saturday went to Regents Park College soirée. On Sunday went to Walworth to hear Spurgeon, after service walked with Kidd and we got lost, got down the Old Kent Road and had to take horse omnibus, today waited for Mr Stephens till 12½. I went with Randall to station and had to wait at Chalk Farm butchers shop for bus. It was raining hard and after a few enquiries found the humble cottage where our dear friends were living. Mr Stephens had started out to fetch me and didn't return until I was there, we then went to see his Tabernacle. Poor Mrs Stephens is in deep sorrow, she is going next week into hydropathic institution at Royston and hopes great things may be accomplished by it.

Wed 24th   This morning Charles and I went to business. Called on Thurston and found him cool as he didn't get copper shares for us, but had for Kidd. So we got what monies we could and succeeded pretty well. We dined at Anchor and I returned to tea, then met Brooks under rostrum and had serious thoughts on seeing Spurgeon.[28] It was first time I had seen him since I saw him at dear Papa's deathbed at Maize Pond in Bermondsey. After supper Mr Wassell seemed very serious with Charles. Henry Wassell arrived unexpectedly this afternoon. He looks a thorough fop.

Thurs 25th   Henry breakfasted here. Mr Wassell, Kingdon and I went to Easter Hall and there met Uncle B.T., Mr and Mrs Stephens and

Mrs Beal. Syckleman said I was so thin and pale he hardly knew me.
Was excited to speak to Spurgeon again and he remembered his visit
to dear Papa on his deathbed. After dining, Kingdon chaperoned me
to Paternoster Row to look at books. After supper Mr Brown visited
and was pleased to see us, he said his visit to Fairford was one of the
most interesting he ever had. He asked if Kate and I would be going
to Jamaica. I wondered at his saying so. Went to Albion Chapel and
saw Earl Shaftesbury present Baumann and Bonhon, missionaries,
with a bible each. Was much disgusted with Hill's conduct when
prayer was proposed. He, Mostyn and Henry Wassell had been laughing and wanted to put prayer aside altogether. Mr Philips had to
reprove them.

Sat 27th   Very snowy so couldn't go to Grays. Wassell left at 5 this
morning for Bath and Sarah at 6 for Saffron Walden. It is dull here
with Henry, so try to avoid him. Kidd calls every day.

Mon 29th   Heard from dear Kitty. She said that Hannah had told her
that dear J had row with Belchers. He had kissed one of the servant
girls in fun and they had made a handle of it. All this wants me to
break up our connexion. Kidd called and came with Charles and me to
get dividends. Charles went on to do more business and Kidd took me
to Anchor to dine off salmon and jam pudding, he then took me to
Wheeler's, bought pair best kid gloves for me and one for Kate,
bought me little bottle of stuff for hair which costs 1/6 and a scent
box for 1/-, though I demurred at every purchase. He then vexed me
by ordering cab to take me to his old lodgings at Holloway, though I
had no chaperone, I had wanted to visit Mrs Thomson and go to worship, but he was full of his fun. Ordered tea then said he gets increas-
ingly fond of me and thinks he shall have me for his wife. Thank you
not, Sir!!!

Tues 30th   At 12 I left for Grays. Charles waited to see drawing of
prizes at Art Union so came first. Ordered leg of mutton by Kidd's
direction at Potters and fly to be at station 7$^1/_2$, and here I am at Grays
writing in Kidd's library, all alone in my glory. Walked here with
butcher's boy and he amused me telling me how he had been thrown
out of car though not seriously hurt. Charlotte brought me nice new
bread and butter and sherry wine and lighted good fire. Then I dined
at 5 off the leg, and very good it was, finished up with rhubarb tart.
Charles arrived at 6, two hours later than he had said, he was disappointed at not getting prize, but revived after dinner. Then Kidd came

at 7 to dine, then we tead after I had been with Charlotte to see ducks. Kidd wouldn't believe how Charles and Randall made a hat gallop round by turning it on the table when they were at Randall's last night, so had fun trying to turn it again.

MAY

Wed 1st Very restless night. Got up at 4 and re-made my bed. Kidd left for town before we were up, but had left a job gardening for us both. I put seeds in and Charles pruned trees. Dined at 1 and left at 2 having enjoyed it, except for disappointment at not going to Liberation soirée as we came back on purpose to go, but Charles declined because he would not change his shirt, though 'twas black. I thought it unkind of him to disappoint me over such a trifle as putting on a clean shirt and I would not go with him in a dirty one. A company of Bedford choir arrived last night and sung today at Crystal Palace, 3,000 attended. In evening they sang to us. I admired their voices greatly. Kidd came in and I noticed he was very free with one of them.

Thurs 2nd Charles and I went to Thurstons to finish business at bank. Kidd came in evening and staid night, he makes us have port wine hot every night.

Fri 3rd A nice warm day. Charles treated Kidd and self to dinner at Anchor. It cost him 4/8d. Then I walked to Islington and tead at Thomsons.

Sat 4th The weather bitterly cold. More intense than all winter. We left at 6½. Martha Bedwell, as was, came down too and said John's wife would be at Swindon and they were going to Kempsford. I went to see the Town Hall at Swindon. Charles took me to the bar, but didn't make himself very agreeable, I shall be glad to get back to dear Kate. Hannah met us at Cirencester and was pleased to see my dear Kitty looking quite well.

Mon 6th Much warmer today. While I was gardening John arrived. I had such confused thoughts and emotions on seeing him again as yesterday Kate had told me much that she has heard of him. She said there seems to be a very unkind spirit about him, and some untrue things said, but I fear that it is levity which has given rise to much. Mrs Frise insisted we all went to sup, the evening was pleasant enough but Charles staid smoking till midnight.

Tues 7th   John very orderly. I talked to him about reports. He cleared it up, but seems too indifferent as to what others may think of his conduct. I spoke very plainly to him, and I fear he is not very spiritual. After early tea I took him and Hannah halfway to Arlington, and it began to pour so heavily with rain that he walked on alone and I brought Hannah back with me. We called on Mrs Radway and paid her bill. Miss Beach was married today.

Wed 8th   Another wet and cold day. Couldn't manage to meet Mr King at Cirencester, so he came by Brasington's pony chaise before tea, which put us about a bit as we expected him to come by Collett's carrier's cart. But 'twas alright. He was very glad to see us, said Kate looks better and thought I looked better and younger also.

Fri 10th   Such a sharp frost, cistern iced over, potatoes and vines all cut. Anxious at not having news of Alice and Ellen. Went to Park gardens yesterday it being fine. Poor Mrs Savory very ill.

Mon 13th   Mr King, having preached for Mr Frise, staid the night and Charles had difficulty in getting horse to drive him back to Cirencester. Kate and I went too. It is the first time that Kate has been so far for so long. The Keyworths were so pleased to see her. We went to Berry's about our bonnets. When we got back to tea at Keyworths Mrs William Coles was there, very friendly, she couldn't help telling us that her Bessie was engaged, but spoke strongly against married life. Parr came when we got home and I had interesting talk with him on baptismal regeneration. He speaks very sensibly, but though he wouldn't consent, he allowed his wife to have his children christened.

Tues 14th   This is Fair Day.²⁹ Ten weeks have passed and still no tidings of The Wilton. We are more and more anxious about Alice and Ellen and I posted to Mr East trying to make the best of it.

Thurs 16th   Busy gardening. Mr Cornwall said Sam Peters wished to come to Quenington but couldn't hear of house. I directly thought he might take ours for a time and wrote at once to name it to Mrs Yells and then named it to our Heavenly Father. I wonder which will reply first, I patiently await the result. Uncle and Aunt Thomas called this afternoon. They were very agreeable. Aunt B.T. has not been in this house for many, many years. I never recollect seeing her here more than once, when I was quite a child. Mr Smith called for his preaching dues, and we paid him £6 5s to Lady Day.

Sun 19th   The good news come at last. Miss Thomson wrote to say that yesterday morn the post brought her a letter from Alice East off Lizard Point, and Kidd, in answer to this note, says The Wilton was sighted off Dartmouth, short of provisions, but had now been supplied and proceeded to harbour.

Mon 20th   Kate still poorly. I went to East End Surgery and paid Mr Cornwall to 1861 a total of £26 5s. Miss J Iles and Mrs Reynolds here for Dorcas meeting. Tea meeting at Crofts Hall (Reynolds). I went with Mrs Frise. Mr Stafford preached in evening and came home with me to sup.

Wed 22nd   Heard from Alice and Ellen, poor girls they began to think they should never reach London, their journey has taken 11 weeks. Heard yesterday from Mr Wassell to say that if we do let our house he thinks Mrs's cousin, Mr Whitaker would be likely to take it for a time. Mrs Coles came to tea and Sam to sup. They thought our garden looks very nice, they wonder how we keep it and the house as well as we do, they were delighted with the study. Charles not well, worked too long in the hot sun yesterday. Uncle B.T. called, invited us all to dine at St John's Bridge for the anniversary of their wedding day.

Sat 25   Have not heard anything further on our letting house, not even Mrs Yells, so I wrote to Wassells about it.

Mon 27th   Mr Yates and Frise exchanged pulpits, then he preached at Kempsford yesterday afternoon. Emma asked leave to go to the Primitives, I was sorry, but agreed to it. Showed Mr Yates new building and study. He left by Collett. Parr sent some dahlias. Heard from Wassells that they don't think the cousin will be coming, then Mrs Yells wrote that Mr Peters also declined through illness of an aunt.

Wed 29th   Charles drove me to Meysey Hampton as I was short of time having worked hard and long in the garden. Took few eggs to Ann Truman and ham and wine to Sarah Short. Found latter very sadly and weak also her aunt. My heart was melted as I compared their sufferings with our mercies I felt humbled and grateful. Mary Miller says she owes her religious convictions to the instruction she received at Sunday School at Meysey Hampton. Mrs Bedwell came to tea, she is broken hearted at the loss of her husband. The Hewers kindly sent a rabbit for the loan of coat and bonnet.

❧ JUNE ❧

Sun 2nd   Wassells wrote again to say that the cousin declined our house being so inaccessible by rail.[30] Charles muttered into his pipe again about it as he has worked hard to forge the matter of railway to Fairford. Kate and I went to baptizing over the way. The chapel was full but the children very noisy. Bess Payne, Bess Edwards, Mr Sly and Mr Barrett were baptized. Kate and I intended to remain and commune with them as the Lord's Supper was administered, but Mr Frise did not invite us to do so, so we rose and sat on the other side.

Mon 3rd   Very busy all day. Mr Shepherd supped here. He sat until ¼ to midnight, though his wife begged him not to stay as her sister is very ill, and delirious. Ellen Booker called on her pony and I walked part of the way home with her, gathered wild flowers and made nosegay of them, was delighted to hear the nightingale.

Thurs 6th   Again B.T. made me vexed over horse. Eventually got ours back from him then had to send to Richard to come from Halls to drive for us. Mrs Rose couldn't come till today and the washing doesn't dry. Called on Tom Clarke and he gave his mother the long promised tea and sugar, got Mary Miller alone and spoke to her most seriously about marrying an unconverted man, she says that several have warned her against it, so I think she will consider it again.

Fri 7th   Mrs Burge and Sydney came at 11. Francis drove us to Sheephouse for dinner, then we walked over the farm, saw poultry feeding and after tea had music. Enjoyed the day very much, but fear Kate was too poorly to really enjoy it, she kept very quiet. Returned at 10½.

Sun 9th   Francis drove us to Arlington. Went to chapel with Mrs Belcher. Didn't expect to see John as Charles had said he was at Randalls. Didn't have time to say more than 'How dye do'. He sat in pulpit long time after service, but came later to sup and then as I was leaving, he jumped into coburg to ride a little way back with me. I felt glad on all accounts. Saw Mr Smith's young lady at chapel, Miss Powell, just like him.

Mon 10th   Kate went to Uncle's to see to how we should be expected to go tomorrow as Mrs Albert Iles had called and I had to discuss with her about Burges. She asked if Burge was under any restrictions as to underletting. Mrs Iles and family wish to come here and find Burge doesn't give up key till Midsummer's Day. I told her that Charles would not wish to prevent their coming. They hire furniture from Brown for a few weeks.

Tues 11th Made up pretty bouquets for Uncle and Aunt and culled my choicest flowers. Made screen of writing paper for the back of them and Kate tied them on with white ribbon. She, poor girl, was so poorly I feared she wouldn't be able to go so gave her some hot grog and she recovered in time. I sent the flowers with Emma and they were delighted with them for as they passed our house they flourished them about. Aunt B.T. and Mrs Sturgiss who sat next to her in the carriage, bowed gaily. We followed at 12, Francis drove. They had chosen the Trout Inn at St John's Bridge, Lechlade as that is where they had kept their wedding day 50 years ago today. It was soon evident that something was wrong. It was that we couldn't have the large room on the lawn as it was out of order. Then the room we were to occupy was very, very dusty. The poor old lady seemed sadly mortified as she wanted it to be so nice. I greeted her with a kiss and wished her much happiness. Dinner was ordered for 2, but didn't appear until 2½, Uncle began to growl till Mr Sturgiss begged him act the philosopher's part and not think so much of trifles. When dinner was served up well it put the old gent in good humour. And good it was:

The Trout Inn, Lechlade

boiled salmon trout, fried eels and perch, with which we had a bottle of sherry. This was followed by chicken and ham, plum pudding and tarts, cheese and cucumber and dessert, figs, almonds, raisins and port wine. Several toast were drunk and letters from absentees read. Mont Sturgiss read a few lines of his own composition, then he sung and acted the Cobbler and Shoemaker. Kate and I then had to sing 'The kine, the kine, a boat, a boat' before tea at 6. The horses were ordered for 7½ and all having passed off pleasantly we returned home, Mr Sturgiss riding with us. He made it more lively and we were singing rounds all the way home, but I felt it would have been more appropriate to raise a hymn of praise..

Sat 15th   Weather very warm. Kate and I walked to Furzy Hill. Was disappointed that they did not meet Kate with pony, but after tea and rest, we slowly returned and she bore it pretty well. Emma had her Primitive friend Smith to dine while we were out.

Mon 17th   Kate and I busy making green gooseberry preserve. Frise tuned the piano for us. Felt sadly annoyed that Mr Davis had not been over. I am unhappy when he slights me, yet I cannot decide on furthering the union.

Sat 22nd   Ann Laight came yesterday. It was such a bad thunderstorm that she staid night. She's the same as ever, but we packed her off today with a dark dress, some gooseberries and some plants. Mr Cornwall thinks Kate and I should go to seaside, but there is still the troubles which Charles endeavours to sort out.

Sun 23rd   Had letter from Kidd, he says Wyldes owns to pocketing £200. They think of serving the firm with a writ. Kidd fears they have pawned the title deeds of our tithes and other things. My prayer is that God will defeat their wicked schemes. Then, on going into the orchard this morning, I found a nest of 12 eggs in manger covered over, but I left them there to see what is happening. Mrs Albert Iles called, she walked round the garden and was delighted with it, she said it was the prettiest place in Fairford and asked us to go and see her at The Cottage, up above.

Mon 24th   Not feeling very well, I was lying on sofa after dinner and heard Emma say 'Oh, Mr Davis'. My heart leapt into my mouth and then he came in and shook hands. I was quite overcome and had to leave the room for a while, but it was alright and we later strolled into the garden and across the Green. Dear John, he picked me a nosegay of forget-me-nots from the water's edge, not knowing the name until I said it to him. We tead on the lawn, and afterwards he cut off strawberry suckers. After supper he went alone in the garden to catch moths. Before bed he suddenly warmed up and then became as usual. The excitement knocks me up.

Tues 25th I breakfasted in bed and Kate went down to breakfast with dear J alone. My heart aches over him. He left as Mr Cornwall called to see Kate. It was starting to rain but he refused umbrella and had no coat and only a thin cap. We took a warm leave at the green door. I went to Crofts Hall with Miss J Iles to hear a talk on the Jews.

JULY

Mon 1st Emma was late up. It was 10 o'clock before the hall began to be scrubbed or tea things washed. Poor Kate had to have another blister, but it didn't rise well, not even with the leaves I put on later. I've been busy picking raspberries all day.

Tues 2nd I was in the middle of the big strawberry bed, busily picking, when dear brother Charles returned from London. I was delighted to have him home again and so was Kate. He has served writ on Wyldes firm for £200.

Wed 3rd Mr Keyworth and Lawler drove up after tea, was pleased to hear from them that dear J did not seem to have suffered from walking home in the heavy storm, as they had been to see him about preaching at Cirencester next Sunday and were sending Shepherd to Arlington. I caught several moths and caterpillars for his collection. Have been busy at household accounts and talks with Charles on our financial state.

Mon 8th Mr Cornwall called, he and Susan have been up to London as the poor old chap is quite deaf. He was quite in a growling mood and Susan says it is because he and the London doctors cannot agree on the cause of his deafness. He is anxious for us to get away for sea air that we think of going soon.

Thurs 11th Had the Frises children over for tea and a romp in the orchard with me. They all enjoyed it. While feasting on strawberries, Mrs Keyworth came, then Mr Coles and Sam. It was fun to hear the exclamations of them all at strawberries. They all said they never saw such lots and feasted up to their eyebrows.

Sat 13th   So busy picking and preserving strawberries and currants. Had note from Mr Davis to say he is going to Blockley, so couldn't come to Fairford. I was vexed about it as I had spent a long time catching a dragonfly for him. I wrote by return to say that Kate and I are going to the Isle of Wight next week and sent him the fly, the caterpillars and another moth. I would have liked to go to Croombes's sale next week but we shall be away.

Sun 14th   Mrs Belcher, the Keyworths and children came and we went to chapel. Mr Belcher had gone to Blockley with John. Mrs B says she wishes I would settle and have John. My heart goes out to him, but he will never know it. I feel as though there is now something happening which will make us separate, never to meet as before. I don't think I can ever love anyone else, but I feel he has grown cool. I fear it is all arranged by Providence, but that is what I had sought – a firm direction. But I do love the dear fellow though.

Fri 19th   After busy time bottling fruit and preparing for journey, we left yesterday at 8. Charles kept us late at breakfast. We reached Trowbridge soon after 12. Went into pastry cook's shop for refreshments having to wait 3 hours. Heard of some of my old schoolfellows and we explored the town. Mr Penny met us at Bradford and Mrs Wassell was running about as if nothing was up. Miss Groves was here from Bath until 6. This morning (Friday) Mrs Penny came into our room to say that Mrs Wassell would not be up for breakfast as she was not feeling well. Dr Highmore came at 9 and at a little before 10 Mrs Penny came to say there was a fine little girl. 'Twas all over while we were at breakfast. Aunt Penny seemed to want it all to herself this time, though Mrs Wassell had said she was expecting us, but she didn't send to us in her labours as she didn't think either of us would be well enough to bear it, so thought it best if we amused Mr Wassell downstairs while she got on with it. He was delighted with his little girl.

Sat 20th   Sarah Wassell came at 8 from Bath and when we walked in garden she said she was engaged to a gent in Bristol, and all were much pleased with it. She left again at 8 in the evening and we went to station with her.

Wed 24th   I have been happy enough without Mr Davis since I've been here and think my mind is now set to be thinking less of him, although all are anxious to know the situation. Had a nice walk by the canal. Mrs Wassell seems sadly.

Fri 26th   Mr Wassell had letter from Mr Coomber asking if he might pay attention to Miss Wassell. This, when he is engaged to her, it was strange and there was an odd expression in it about he didn't want to pay idle visits. Kate had letter from friend Susan Cornwall, she urges us to get on to seaside.

Sat 27th   Walked round the garden with nurse, she told us strong things about Mr Penny, says he pretends to eat nothing hardly and he's so deceitful to eat heartily many times a day when no one sees him. He also has his cup of beer often, though he never touches more than water in front of others. He watered nurse's beer, and strange to say our porter was watered, I noticed it straight away. I could not drink it at all.

Sun 28th   Kate and I went to chapel and met Mr and Mrs Newell. He told us that there was a man there called White who had been baptized in Ganges either by Carey or our grandfather Thomas,[31] but he was now a backslider.

Mon 29th   Sarah came again from Bath. I thought her hoop quite outrageous. She thought it made her look attractive. I can see that Mr Coomber's salary of £250 is a great salvo. I was very busy making up baby's cap and trimming hood.

❧ AUGUST ❧

Fri 9th   We were pleased with the little we saw of Portsmouth. Going to Ryde we had unusually rough voyage being a brisk wind. Saw two or three quite ill. I nearly so and poor Kitty looked so pale before we landed. It was a great comfort to have Mr King with us as he looked to everything nicely. At Ryde there was a rush, coaches soon filled up with Ventnor passengers. We had to stand an hour and a half before we could get anything. A gent arrived on next boat and joined us in carriage for 7/-, thus reducing it to 5/-. Mrs Goodfellow received us most kindly and made us at once feel at home. Tea was waiting on the table and we felt refreshed after some. We all walked on the sands after. Mrs Goodfellow's mother and sister are here, which we regret. The sisters sang and played in evening.

Sat 10th   Mr King sleeps next door at Dunns. Went for walk, but Miss Tomkins, Mrs G's sister insisted on accompanying us to our annoyance.

Sun 11th   Mr King came for us and we went to church. It was crowded. In afternoon we went to the re-opening of the little Independent chapel. Mr Beresford spoke, he said much that was objectionable and little of profit and was very pompous. Later Mr King and Mr Saunders took us to where Mr King was to address navvies. Mr Saunders so reminded us of Captain Milbourne that we couldn't help smiling as he gave out the hymn sheets.

Mon 12th   Kate and I went to baths. Kate had a tepid one. After tea we all went for walk over cliff, again *they* putting forward to come, so that we couldn't refuse without being rude. As we walked on we heard a noise of rumbling and directly met some ladies and a gent who advised us to go no further as a quantity of cliff had fallen.

Tues 13th   Again did that Lucy intrude, coming to us while preparing and asked that she might come too. We had pony and trap and went to Shanklin Chine. We much enjoyed it. Paid boy 1/6 and sent him back. Very tired when we left the Chine so we went to Chine Inn and had a glass of brandy and water between us and a biscuit. Walked home on the sands.

Wed 14th   Sad that Mr King had to leave this morning. Mrs Goodfellow is anxious that Charles shall come and buy a house here for us to live in. I have an idea it would be a good idea to invest a little money in land here and looked at a house and garden for £700 with that in view. Kate and I had a bathe in sea. She bore it well enough and afterwards I gave her a thorough rubbing to make her warm.

Thurs 15th   While writing in our room we were summoned down to help decorate the National School room ready for the navvies tea this evening. A Mr Watney from Clapham Park Hill is prime mover in it. I made a crown and helped Mr Watney lay the tables. He is a most active and devoted young man. Some 250 navvies came and conducted themselves in the most orderly manner. In each place was laid a printed grace to be said before and after meat, and on that a pretty bouquet on a background of white paper. They had a good tea: a mutton pie for each man and cake and bread and butter besides. There were speeches and prayers and hymns and psalms between each part of the meal. A short prayer was printed for every man with a little piece of blue ribbon through the middle to hang it up by and also a little book 'A Saviour for You'. One poor man rose on behalf of all and thanked the friends for their kindness. Two policemen were stationed at the door, but there was happily not the least occasion for their services. We were startled this morning hearing of the three Miss McCleans. They were out bathing and got out of their depth, were frightened and screamed. The bathing man went to their rescue on a horse and brought them in safely. A doctor bathing next to them also went to their aid. Miss Boon saw it all from her shop door.

Sat 17th   Kate had another little bathe. Heard from Charles this morning to say that B Thomas and Mr Pinnell called to know if we would let our house for a term of years for £50 and we must answer by return, but I could tell Charles did not like it and therefore would not like to do so. Mrs Goodfellow too poorly to dine with us, they fear a miscarriage. Did not enjoy the family prayer this evening at home, hymns sung so low and slow that I could only think of 'Hosannas languish on our tongues and our devotions die'. Heard that 5 feet nothing was at Shanklin Chine a few minutes after we were. He had just completed tour round the island and returned to Southampton with Mr King.

Mon 19th   Lucy, unasked, went with us to walk towards Culver cliffs. We were much startled to hear a bullet whizz past our heads. The riflemen were practising on sands below. That is the second time we have just escaped, each time when we have had bad thoughts about that Lucy joining us. Mrs Goodfellow is so nice in contrast, she is anxious that we should come here for 12 months. She wishes me to be her sister-in-law, says I should be just the one for her brother Henry. He is coming here soon and she wants us to meet him.

Wed 21st   In an attempt to become more friendly with Lucy as we do not want to tempt Providence to punish us, Kate and I had two machines drawn up close to hers when we went bathing. There was much swell in the water and my teeth didn't stop chattering for half an hour.

Thurs 22nd   Mrs Goodfellow, being so much better, came with Kate and me to Bradford cemetery which is very pretty and kept in good order. It spoke of peace and repose and almost invited one to slumber there. The lad who drove the pony and trap then took us to church to see 'Little Jane's grave' and the graves of the poor woman and those of her children, murdered by their father who was insane. He attempted then to murder himself but was discovered and survived a short time. We paid the lad 1/6d and he returned with pony. After sitting on the grass to eat biscuits and apples we walked home to late tea. In the evening we had music and singing.

Fri 23rd　I was very poorly in evening with pain in back, was obliged to lie on floor in kitchen. Mrs Goodfellow very kind but old Mrs Tomkins and that silly Lucy looking on, I wished them far away. Poor old lady gave us a fine treat earlier, she growled sadly at every meal, quarrelled with every word that was spoken and was very dictatorial, but we let her have her own way and it wore itself out. Often when I feel annoyed with her I think of our own dear mother and it compels me to forbear. She always taught us to reverance old age. How often I wish I could tell her how much I owe to her kind teaching, but I fear I am more sensible of it now than I was when she was here.

Sat 24th　The weather is now lovely and the evenings are splendid. The moon shining over the sea is more beautiful than I can describe. Charles forwarded letter from John and William, they talk of returning from Australia, have lost part of £250. Was delighted to hear from Charles saying that he shall probably be one amongst the next who will be baptized at Meysey Hampton.

Thurs 29th　The days have been spent in lovely weather. Mr Henry Goodfellow was expected by omnibus and many rose during tea to see the conveyances every time we heard a horse pass, but he didn't come. After tea Kate and I went for a walk, when we returned Mr Henry had arrived and was at supper. I was disappointed in his appearance at once, and he is so quiet.

Fri 30th　Feel very stiff and reserved and constrained before Mr Henry G, I am convinced he has been joked about me. He too seems constrained and steals some sly glances across the table at me. Mrs Goodfellow proposed we go to Black Gang Chine, so set to and helped cut sandwiches. We couldn't but take Mrs Tomkins and Lucy with us. The ride was lovely. We had a waggonnette for the day: man and horses for £1 1s. Our share 7/-. We walked a little of the way for the sake of sea view, Bonchurch was our chief delight. Such fairyland. It was most picturesque. The first and last time we came was with Miss Macauley and Mrs Milbourne. We stopped at St Lawrence's Well for horses to drink and then we ran up to the church, truly it is a tiny affair of it. We dismounted at the Chine, through bazaar close to the Inn, saw skeleton of whale caught near there. We sat down and had our sandwiches, had some good porter and went down the very narrow and very steep path, leaving Mrs Tomkins to rest. Only a slight rope was there to hang on to. We sat on shingles and ate biscuits and greengages, the latter brought by Mr Henry Goodfellow. The waves tossed themselves in a very saucy manner. I gave some tracts to a little boy and asked him to pray to God to make him a good little boy. The rocks were 900 feet above us, but I felt a little disappointed in it. Mr Henry helped me up, but had little to say. When we returned the Master of the bazaar poured eau-de-cologne on our handkerchiefs to refresh us, and we bought some little things there. Wished Charles here to enjoy it with us.

Sat 31st Capt Estmann called just as we were going out. Oh, I lifted up my heart to God and asked him immediately to order my steps as Mr Henry G, Capt M and even dear J were put in the background a once. I prayed that if He thought fit He should put affection in Capt Estmann's heart for me. In the evening Mr Henry proposed a walk to Kate and me, then took charge of me, but I never could love him, though he is very kind and they all here wish for the union. The sun set brilliantly and cast a lovely pink reflection from one end of the bay to the other. I never saw anything like it before.

SEPTEMBER

Sun 1st In evening Capt Estmann came to prayer meeting then we all went to outdoor preaching. Saw Mrs West sitting on heap of stones so I took her out thick shawl to wrap around her, she was most grateful and I saw that Capt E noticed it. He then addressed the navvies and afterwards we all went for a walk. Mr Henry very kind and attentive to me, he keeps close to get me to walk with him, but I rather avoid him, he gathered seaweed for me. I could hardly keep my eyes from Capt E, but later that evening I overheard Mrs Tomkins saying that Capt Estmann 'is subject to derangement'. Thus ends all thoughts of him.

Tues 2nd Rose early to finish packing but the day was one of adventure. Sought Mr Griffiths to cord the two boxes and put the labels close by each box. Lo and behold when we had breakfasted and went up to put on our bonnets saw one box untouched. Could find no one and the horses at the door. It was quite a bustle for Kate and me to get the box done in time. Mr and Mrs Goodfellow and Mr Henry rode with us to Ryde. Met Benjamin Harrison and had to hastily question him as to qualifications for our service, having heard of his piety and that he wishes to obtain situation with Christians, but 'twas all bustle and they hurried us on to the boat. Mr Henry very kind and took my arm and hurried us on. We were sad at parting with kind Mrs Goodfellow, but not so her mother and sister. When the boat slipped away from the pier Kate said the bonnet box was left at Inn, a man pushed it in because a little rain was falling and we forgot about it in the bustle. Mr Goodfellow said he should see that the two boxes were put on board, but as we turned to wave adieu the vessel was off and there stood our hapless boxes on the pier, the poor Goodfellows looked dismayed. I was so much so that I could not speak, then turned round and saw poor Mr Henry Goodfellow trying to make an unsuccessful attempt to leave the boat to go ashore. This greatly excited my visible faculties and between the two instances knew not whether to laugh or cry. The former predominated. On reaching Portsmouth Mr Henry left us and kindly promised to deal with the boxes, leaving notice at every station where we could change, *six of them*, for them to be forwarded. We travelled at one stage with a young lady with her invalid sister. We were shocked to hear from her that she had lost her mother and father, brothers and sisters to the number of 12 and most of them in decline. The remaining sister with her is in deep decline too. I asked her if her sister knew of her danger and she said she did, so I gave her one of the little books from the navvies tea gathering, we left the melancholy sight at the next station and I offered up a silent prayer for her salvation. At Cirencester we were met by Charles, and he had Alice East with him. I thought she looked older than I expected. She was 22 last March (1861). When we got home all seemed well. Ellen East, I thought, seemed affected, but I was glad to see them both.

Wed 4th   No luggage by Collett to our disappointment. Susannah and Rachel Cowley called and the latter tead here. It was interesting to go over old times with them. I've not seen her for many, many years when she left in disgrace. Mrs Frise called to see us, she has been quite ill.

Thurs 5th   Mrs Goodfellow wrote to say they took our boxes to carriers' warehouse and had them registered and we should get them in two days. It sadly vexed us as they might have been sent on next boat free of cost.

Fri 6th Alice says they heard in Jamaica before they left that I was to be married to Capt Milbourne. He had told Mrs Troop so. She laughed too about Mr Davis, she said that he and Miss Smith joked very much at a party at Mrs Cook's and she and Ellen were surprised at them both. They then made a tease about him and me and I felt quite annoyed, but it only helps me to give him up. I shall think no more of him for I don't like so much trifling and nonsense. Alice said that he won't be much respected if he goes on like that. Our luggage arrived this morning by Keylock. It cost 8/-. It does vex me as it needn't have been so.

Sat 7th Kate and I took verbena cuttings. Charles told me that when he reached Cirencester he was told that Mr Iles is coming to be a medical partner with Mr Cornwall and wants our house, but it must be kept a strict secret. We declined.

Mon 9th The days have passed much as usual. We are much attached to dear Alice. Ellen has now decided she likes to be called Nelly – she is volatile.

Wed 11th Mr Frise called this morning. Alice, Nelly, Kate and self tead at Mrs Burges. Alice and Nelly say Capt Milbourne was insistent that he was to marry me and folks believed it. Then, as if by chance, Charles had a letter from the Capt. He is coming to England in March, says he would like a ramble with Charles in the summer and will write again when he has any interesting missionary accounts to give.

Fri 13th The weather is most lovely. Harvest gathered in admirably. This evening went to chapel for thanksgiving for the fine harvest, but very few out.

Tues 17th Last Sunday we went to church to hear the Rev Mr Rice. No Mr D since our return, for that I am glad now as I have not the least wish to see him. We walked to Furzy Hill to tea. Miss Eaglesfield and Lewis, her lover, were there. We were all amused by Tom's queer speeches. He said when Mr Williams and all were present, 'Miss Thomas, Mr Williams thinks I've got worms.' Ellen greatly vexed me, directly she saw Lewis she fixed her eyes on him and looked stead-fastly at him nearly all evening. I could not have believed it of her and I never saw any girl do so before. Her looks quite shocked me, but they gained their purpose and made Lewis slight his lady and flirt with her. She said she had a headache and left the room about 7. We saw her no more. Charles came for us and we walked home after supper, Lewis with Ellen, and Gerring with Kate. I spoke to Alice about Ellen's looks and she had noticed it too and was much grieved. I felt disgusted at the little hussy and know the others noticed it too.

Wed 18th Alice told Ellen of her conduct and she has been so good and proper all day that I could not remain angry with her, but she has a high spirit. She was most put out last Sunday when her Papa's letter came urging them beware of the flattering attentions of worldly young me and the snares of the evil one. He proposed their return to Jamaica in November. Had he seen her last night he might well be afraid of her. If she indulges in it she will get into trouble.

Thurs 19th Susan Cornwall called. She said her father had seen Kate in Brown's shop this morning and went to speak to her and she was most haughty, so Sarah came to find out what was the matter. We did not say much about it.

Wed 25th Was much taken to yesterday when Emma suddenly told Kate she wanted to leave at Michaelmas. While busy in the kitchen this morning I spoke to her about it and she said she liked us very much and would stay if we could get someone to clean the knives and forks. She said some young people are trying to get her back to Cirencester but she thinks it might be foolish to leave. We agreed to go on as we are. Comley drove H Harries and the two Miss Clappens from Cirencester and Mr Jones. At last we saw Mr Jones. Alice has told me all her heart about him. She is very fond of him and thinks he is of her, but he takes little notice of her in company. He is very lame, having a cork leg. He is very ordinary and rather blunt in manner. Is hurt that Frise didn't invite him last week to tea meeting. A big company assembled and Mr Davis came and seemed a little excited I thought, but so many there we couldn't speak until after everyone had gone from here after supper. I left Alice and Mr Jones to talk alone in back parlour, then John got warmed up before bedtime, he staid the night but so many here he behaved perfectly.

Thurs 26th A lovely day, warm and sunny. Alice, Ellen, Kate and John and self walked through the grove and back home by the lodge. I was sadly vexed to discover from their talk that while I was upstairs at prayer John had tried to kiss Ellen and she refused in fun and ran up the servants' stairs at the back, he followed her and they wrestled on

The Woodhouse, Alfred's Hall, Cirencester Park

the landing and Emma heard and saw it all and told Kate about it this morning. I was annoyed with John for being so foolish. He is so light and trifling. I know there's too much occasion for it, though Ellen ought to be the last to speak of it since she's always trifling with Ellen Coles at chapel, and Ellen Coles no professor. They laugh and talk at prayer meetings.

Fri 27th Again a lovely day. We all rose early and started for the Woodhouse with Savory's horse in our coburg, as we had sent two teams to Cirencester. Met with friends and they rode behind. Met up with the Keyworths and Sarah Mary at Pope's seat[32] and it was 1 o'clock when we arrived at Woodhouse. We then dined and walked to ten ridings, except Mr Jones who stayed to smoke. After tea we played French Tag, all joined in except Jones as he could not with his cork leg. We felt much disgust because as he smoked he spat on the floor in Woodhouse. Charles smoked with him, but walked to the door to spit. John seemed rather quiet and moody and I discovered later that Kate had spoken to him on his trifling with young people and the harm he did himself over it. He joined in the fun though and enjoyed himself properly.

Sun 29th My mind is unsettled still, I think much of dear J. Half inclined to accept him as I feel much pleasure in his company, but shrink from his trifling ways. Emma very poorly, sent her to bed early having put her feet in mustard water. I warmed her bed and gave her a mixture of honey, vinegar, rum and laudanum. She slept quite soundly after. Francis went to every inn in Cirencester to enquire after our friends the Goodfellows as were expecting them to come today.

❧ OCTOBER ☙

Tues 1st Heard from the Goodfellows that the sea was too boisterous to make the crossing, so now they would come on their way from London. Mr Parr called and talked with Charles about taking his land, making it a nursery. We fear B.T. gains too much by Charles to let him go if he can help it. Mr Parr brought me many verbena cuttings. Mrs Frise tead here and Sam Burge supped. He is rather too familiar in his manner.

Thurs 3rd We had been stewing all day not knowing the Goodfellows' address in London, however, in they came by coach, coming by venture as they had not received our letter. I went after tea with them for walk in the park. While gardening I caught a beautiful humming bee moth without injury, first by throwing my hat over it and pressing the brim closely while Kate ran for some gauze to spread over it. I put glass over it and Kate wrote to John to ask if he would like it for his collection. Alice and Nelly in Cirencester visiting friends but returned tonight. Alice is sadly as Mr Jones had bid her a final adieu as it will go no further now. Sam Burge came over to see Nelly as soon as they returned. Poor Alice, I sat in her bedroom as I could see she was upset over Mr Jones, and I told her of dear Ma's death. We then wept on each others necks. I love dear Alice very much and she loves us, she would very much like to settle in England. Nelly not at all well.

Mon 7th Uncle B.T., Charles and Nelly went to Cirencester Mop[33], though the latter was professing not to be well enough to attend chapel yesterday, which brought remarks from Emma. Alice would not have gone to Mop even if they had asked her. She and I lit a fire in the back parlour and played music.

Tues 8th I took Alice and Nelly down to the Cornwalls to bid them adieu. Mrs Cornwall asked to speak to me, she is afraid that we are cross with Mr Cornwall and that we sought medical advice for Kate in Bradford. We did not and I tried to assure her that it was us that were hurt as he did not call as often as he might. Then Susan came and asked me to go into orchard and she started it all over again. I gave our united love to him through Susan and said we should be very pleased to see him again. Later, Charles drove us to Arlington and John was at Belchers when we arrived. He brought his cases of moths and butterflies for us to see. They do him great credit. I felt rather constrained as last night Alice said that she wondered I didn't keep him at greater distance if my mind was made up to reject him. I felt the truth of it for when I see him I find great difficulty in keeping him at a distance. Charles enjoyed dear J's preaching and my heart was lifted, but then John joined us to come little way home, he started his old tricks and when he knew Alice was no longer in thought of Mr Jones he said 'I think I'll stick up for Alice, she seems a very nice girl.'

Wed 9th Emma went home today for a week's holyday. Mr Jones came by Collett quite unlooked for and wanted to see Frise. I could soon tell that he thinks nothing of Alice for wife, though he likes her well enough.

Fri 25th Numerous engagements have prevented my adding to these notes till today. We managed very nicely while Emma was home. Mrs Wall came to clean up and got everything in nice clean order, Emma noticed it when she returned on Tuesday. Mr Cornwall came, said but little and left early. He badly wants us to go on as before and we said we are happy to do so, Susan called later and told me much about matter between her father and Mr Iles, who wants to go into practice with him at their East End surgery. She told me things she could not tell another creature beside me. On 13th we heard from dear Alice to say they went to Blockley and they were then called to London to see Grandma who was taken suddenly ill. I wrote short note to Mr Davis enclosing bill for the tea meeting. We've been to Meysey Hampton often on visits to very sick and the poor, but when I saw Sarah Short I was struck by a most pitiable sight. Her face is quite destroyed by disease, only one side is at all like a human face and the smell is sickening. It made me feel sick and faint for some time. I thought that when Mr Rodway spoke at service it was rather too exciting. The tea meeting was very crowded and kept us all busy. Had words about her domestic trials to Mrs Hayward, she says they are weaning her from the world. The Howards arrived, unexpected, as we were at enquirer's meeting and we had to scurry about to make up beds, then in came Mr Rodway expecting a bed, and when he saw how we were all about he was most kind and said he would go to the inn, but we could not hear of it and pulled it all about for him to have another room. 'Twas a scurry and bustle after such a busy day, we were quite knocked up. Uncle B.T. had been up to his usual trick of taking our horses just when we wanted them to take tea things to Meysey Hampton for their meeting. Mr Painter kindly lent us his, but 'twas vexatious. Then we had to get tables taken by Collett's large van. It rained hard so

Kate had to take her dress to change at Hewer's. Harriet had to walk over in the pouring wet to cut up the cake. Charles sorely grieved me by not taking his tea with the others, but carrying it into vestry to have alone. The rain prevented the Arlington and Cirencester folks from coming. Somehow I could not feel such regret at rain as often I should have. It is singular how we always have thunderstorms at Meysey Hampton tea meetings. After the 80 odd people had their tea, Mr Rodway proposed buying all the provisions that were left so that a tea could be given to abandoned characters in Fairford. Miss Iles and Mr Moreton got together a list of indifferent characters and Shepherd was sent round with them.

Sun 27th   We heard that a mason was ill, sent for James Cornwall and he said when he saw him, 'Oh, he's not ill, 'tis these cursed revival meetings, they find more work for the doctors than anything else all over the country.' The man recovered and went to work the next morning. John and Mr Reynolds exchanged pulpits and yesterday when we went to Crofts chapel Mr Reynolds said, 'Now my friends I wish you to pray for our dear brother Davis who will preach here tomorrow.' I hoped a blessing would follow. John slept here but seemed distant.

Mon 28th   Charles went to London by coach. John was very disagreeable all evening, we sat for some time in back parlour without uttering a word, then he argued against Kate and me when we wanted him to ask blessing at table. The Wassells came with baby and nurse to spend a few days, I was glad John went before they arrived but they wished to have seen him. We all had walk in the garden then went into Poole's empty house as Hope wants to take it.

❧ NOVEMBER ❧

Sat 2nd   We thought much of dear Ma, this being the anniversary of her birthday. It is four years since she died. Mr Wassell left by Collett. We had church meeting to receive Edwards back. Of some of those being enquired into I knew nothing of their misdeeds, and said that if the church wished to receive them back I would not oppose it, but it seems as if it was Tom Clarke who urged them back. I've really no faith in them, they express no repentance for the past.

Sun 3rd   We went to Meysey Hampton, baby and all. Called on Mrs Burge, her foot healed up but she is sadly herself.

Park Street, Fairford

Fri 8th Francis drove Mrs Wassell, Kate and I to Arlington. She thought it a lovely drive. We went to see the school and chapel, but nothing of Mr Davis until tea time when he came into Belchers and seemed surprised to see us there. After tea he saw us to the bottom of hill and for first time bid us goodnight there without coming part of the way home with us. The baby was very good, but was frightened of dear J and we all laughed about it. Mrs Wassell spoke to me alone about him after we got home and thinks I am too fastidious. She said she liked him but he's not quite the one she would have chosen for me.

Tues 12th Fair Day. Muddy after frost, but fine. Mr Davis came at 1 o'clock I heard him enter the hall from the orchard without being announced. A little circumstance occurred which vexed me. After dinner I swept up hearth in front parlour and asked John to pass coal box nearer, but in fun he refused to do it, wanting to put coal on himself. I would not let him have the tongs and he would not let me have the coal. We enjoyed the fun, but then he left the room and I thought of how we were both too independent to live happily together. A fire was lit in back parlour and as Emma came in with the tray of tea things she balanced it on her knee to open the door and down went the tray, everything smashed. I could not scold her as she was so sorry and upset. It was Mr Davis who had closed the door as he wanted to talk to me alone. It was not until later that we had half an hour together, and that after Mr Wassell, who arrived by coach at tea time, had nursed the baby and said funny things to dear J about wishing he could see him doing the same. Both the Wassells seem anxious that I should have him, and Mr said that he would give him lessons in perseverance.

Fri 15th   The Wassells left by King for Cheltenham. Mrs Wassell told me that Sarah's wedding could not take place until spring or summer as the house they looked at was too expensive. We thought it queer as her Coombes might easily get less expensive house if that was all. It is quite a relief to us not to be invited to wedding. This I think Mrs Wassell regrets as it is all strangers going. It was quiet when they all left, but Kate and I set to immediately and altered all the beds. Parr brought in the plants and arranged them in little room upstairs.

Sun 17th   This morning heard from Charles that some of the stocks in which Papa invested have sunk 100s in value since then. When Mr Cornwall called yesterday he jumped up as soon as I mentioned religion, but I was only referring to it in connexion with Sarah Short who seems to be sinking sadly.

Sun 24th   Charles home today but has very bad cold. We put his feet in hot mustard bath, warmed his bed and gave him hot rum and honey.

Wed 27th   Susan Cornwall came to tea. We had little music in the evening when Sam Burge came in, but he is very pushing. Then old Parr came to talk to Charles about Burdocks but can't get any settlement over it.

Fri 29th   Parr came again, he is very pushing too, asked Charles to attend meeting this evening at White Hart for purpose of considering if we shall have market here. He went with Parr and brought him back to sup. The meeting agreed to get a market[34] held here.

❧DECEMBER ❧

Thurs 5th   Mr King has been here several days, he, Charles, Emma and I went to Meysey Hampton. After the service I saw Susan Lane and discovered she is very concerned about her unconverted relations. She say she's quite prepared to meet the opposition of her father. She told Mr King she would like to join the church but didn't like one person's conduct there, and was not always struck by the preaching. We had to hold an enquirers' meeting[35] to examine the morals of some members. Found them wanting.

Sat 7th Heard from Mrs Knibb to say she has taken Minnie from school with whooping cough, they will spend Christmas in Northampton and she will bring Minnie here early in January. I look forward to meeting the child with mixed emotions and wonder what her father, Capt Milbourne has told her of his plans for seeking my hand. Susan Cornwall has gone to Partis College. Money markets and bank stocks are all very low in consequence of the reported war with America owing to Stidell and Mason[36] being seized by confederate man-o-war, when on our mail steamer Trent.

Sun 8th My birthday again come round. This morning had letter and locket from E McMichael and letter from Emily. Mrs Mitchell called and seems not a happy woman. She threw out hints of Giles Vincent's unsuitability for membership of Meysey Hampton chapel, this must be cleared up.

Wed 11th This is the day for sale of Charles's tithes in London. Poor fellow, he seems much perplexed and it makes him moody. I have prayed that God will defeat the wicked counsel of his opponents who try to cheat him. Kate and I called on Aunt B.T. who is very poorly. Took her some port wine jelly.

Fri 13th The ill tidings of the tithes unsold came this morning by Kidd. The highest bid was £5,100, I felt discouraged. I can only take comfort in that God defeated the counsels of Ahithophel, so He can in His own good time defeat the wicked devices of Wyldes and Whitehead. Kidd says Fowler is in treaty with a party privately now and I still hope they may be sold. Kate and I took poor Charles for a walk with the little dog, which gave him some amusement.

Sat 14th Heard from dear Alice, she seems to cling to us. Kate and I called on Miss Iles, she made us take a glass of wine. While we were there Mr Cornwall came to see one of the young lady boarder scholars. Wrote to Eliza and sent her a piece of ribbon for neck. Have not heard from dear J as to whether he is coming to spend Christmas here. Charles wishes much I could accept him and so does Kate, but both are very slow in urging it much. The two volumes of Old English History came last night, £3 3s. was paid and it included a fine picture of Westminster Palace.

Mon 16th *Death of Prince Albert.* This morning when Charles went to collect beer from Henry Faulkes, he gathered the news that Prince

Albert is dead! At first we hoped 'twasn't true, but at night the papers confirmed the melancholy news. News quickly spread through London and at midnight the great bell of St Paul's, which tolls alone for Kings and Queens, boomed out its doleful tidings to the inhabitants of London, which expression was quickly followed by all the other church bells continuing for the most part through the night. Every heart must join in this painful event. It is a very sudden shock to the nation. My heart yearns for the Queen.

Wed 18th   The news in papers is very foreboding. The government in America will grant no satisfaction whatsoever to England for seizure of Stiddell and Mason, and war with America seems more than probable. Mrs Hewer sent us a hare and came later to tea.

Fri 19th   Went to see Ann Wall and Nancy Green this morning, gave them both 1/- to get them a Christmas dinner. News of Princess Alice's devotion to her mother is most touching. She made a lovely wreath of flowers to put in Prince Albert's coffin together with a miniature portrait of the Queen, who, as yet, keeps up wonderfully.

Sat 20th   The two eldest Fluxes and Miss Howell called just as we were finishing dinner and evidently hoped to be in time, but we hadn't a morsel left, but gave them some wine and bread and butter, and we three made off into the kitchen to finish our pudding there. Charles went last Thursday to meeting about railway and he took six more shares. It seems sure to come now. Mr Cornwall called this afternoon. I made him have some gingerbread nuts I had just made and a little brandy, which he much liked.

Sun 21st   Weather very cold, looks very threatening for snow. Fearful it will prevent dear J coming, silly thing!! Dread his coming, but dread more his not coming. Shepherd preached at Meysey Hampton to a good congregation. Shocked to hear of Mrs Clissold's sudden death. Charles had letter from Fowler yesterday but did not open it till midday. It was to say the tithes were sold for £5,750 and would leave Charles just what he asked £5,550. It seemed such an answer to my prayer.

Christmas Day: the long looked for come at last. A lovely day. Parr brought some holly and evergreens in, and Charles brought down electric machine, but poor man he was frightened to come near it or us either when we had received a shock. He ran up garden to get away and was glad 'twas church time. Mr Cornwall came unexpectedly, and thereupon came dear J round the lawn. Mr Cornwall said he had seen someone go round but it wasn't Mr Kingsley, naughty man. I believe he came on purpose to see if John came. He asked the other day if I had been to Arlington lately, and had I seen Mrs William Coles. At 4½ we went to tea at the Frises. Left Emma's mother to bear her company, she was driven over by her son in morning. When we returned Emma's mother told me her troubles. She said she and her sister, ages 8 and 10, were turned out of doors by step mother and had to get their livings. She helped support her sister, then went to service, then to a shop and gent fell in love with and married her sister. He died, and the sister forgot the one who had worked and cared for her all those years ago. Mrs Parsons hadn't seen her sister for 40 years and felt it sadly. I gave her a copy of 'The Life of Richard Weaver' which I pray will be a comfort to her.

Thurs 26th Charles said that last night he had his Will[37] signed by Frise and John Davis. This morning the four of us took the two dogs and had a run in the Green. I realise I acted very foolishly throughout the day and I know not why as my heart goes out more to dear J every time we are together, but I joked about my marriage in the Spring and asked dear J if he would come to the wedding. He shook his head sadly and said that from the start I had given him no hope and he had no wish to witness another's happiness at his sorrow. It touched my heart greatly and Kate was vexed with me. She tried to put it right with John by saying that he always teazed me about other girls and his flirtatious ways were the cause of my saying what I did.

Fri 27th I tried hard to keep my equilibrium, but found it difficult, and agitation prevailed. Parr came to talk long time to John then after dinner Charles had romp with me, calling on John to help. He placed his chair close to Kate's and mine then tried to make me sit on it and thus the scuffle as I resisted. However, they conquered me and I afterwards turned round and gave dear J a kiss!! A thing I never did to any gent in the world before!! This, too, when Kate and Charles had left the room. Later, we had a little fun in the hall and he chased me into the front parlour, the arrival of Morty Stephens saved the situation, and dear J had to leave soon after.

Sun 29th Charles and Kate are anxious about me, thinking I look very unwell. Charles said 'it is owing to Mr Davis, and I must now step in and interfere before it injures your health. I shall give him to understand that his visits are not welcome. I have noticed his conduct, which is wanting. I have but one wish and that is to see you happy.' Oh, my heart ached. It is so kind of dear Charles to worry so about me, but I yearn for dear J. Never have I felt so for anyone. If only I could pocket the objections real and fancied and accept him, for I truly love him. I look for signs that he will resort more to the following for which he is practising, but he never talks to me of religious affairs and I fear my own faith will suffer as a result, but he lays these things aside when I talk to him of them. I resorted to reading scripture after scripture and private prayer then went to chapel. There the pulpit was hung all round with black crepe in mourning for Prince Albert, but I felt as though it were for my own heart's loss. I felt quite sick and hurried home after the service, in which I prayed for a double portion of piety and holy zeal to be poured on dear J.

Tues 31st   This is the last day of the year 1861. My mind has been painfully exercised about the useless life I have lived.

1862

⚓JANUARY⚓

Wed 1st New Year's Day! What a volume of mercy does it unfold. I am to see beginning of another year. Kate has a slight relapse and Charles looks so anxious and care-worn that it depresses me. He is worried about giving up the farm. Matters between England and America still threatening. The Times bloodthirsty for war, but sober minded men think it may be averted. This afternoon Charles walked halfway with me to Furzy Hill, met Bessie, but I went on and tead with Ellen and rode pony home, boy leading it carrying lantern.

Fri 3rd Susan Cornwall sitting upstairs when I called, but I didn't stay to tea. Went instead to Mrs Burges to tea and had pleasant evening. I begged her to have family prayers but she says she can't till after her confinement. Letter from Mrs Knibb to say she and Minnie would come on 13th.

Sat 4th Kitty's birthday. I am thankful she is better. Soon after 6 Mr Farr arrived and we had tea. His height quite startled me at first, but his manners are affable and pleasant. He seemed soon to get at home in chat. After supper he gave a long account of smokers and the evil of smoking. In describing the symptoms they answered exactly to what Charles felt when he was taken ill in London when he smoked from morn to night. Charles was rather struck by it and put down his pipe before it was out. He told us that tomorrow he should be 28 years old.

Sat 5th   Mr Farr's birthday. We had Kitty's plum pudding. Mr Farr is 6 ft 5 inches high and was obliged to sit sideways in the pulpit with his feet out at the door. We were obliged to take Papa's travelling cap for him to ride to Meysey Hampton in, as he could not sit in coburg with his hat on. People were all much pleased with his service. I am sadly depressed about my dear brother's appearance he is so sadly neglectful of it. We have spoken of it to him, but he doesn't try to alter it. It is a great grief to dear Kitty also.

Tues 7th   Charles and I went to Cirencester, was most distressed to go up to his room and find him so dirty. Staid tea at Keyworths, Mr Baker, Polly and Eunice there, they promised to come to see us while this moon lasts. On return, went with Mrs Frise to meeting at Crofts Hall.

Thurs 9th   Good news of peace arrived this evening, for which all gave thanks in prayer. The commissioners Riddell and Mason are released. Didn't enjoy prayer meeting, the Primitives as always very loud.

Sun 12th   Went to Meysey Hampton chapel. Tom Clarke wished all enquirers to be present. The ever mean Hannah Vincent and Avis Edwards couldn't speak in the meeting but leant over our pew door to whisper as they went out, 'You were quite right, it ought only to be members to go to tea meeting.' We told them it was wrong to come and say so to us while they didn't name it at meeting. It annoyed me as they thought to please us by it. Uncle B.T. came to say he prevailed upon Charles to give men a supper on Thursday and it was to be held at Mr Faulkes's. In conversation about the land he said, 'You know a part of it is safe to the family and what has been spent will be to their benefit.' Mr Cornwall came while he was here and B.T. said to him rudely 'I expect you have some secrets to talk over.' To our joy he left soon after.

Tues 14th   Charles went to meet coach yesterday, but Mrs Knibb and Minnie came today. Minnie is so like Emma Page that we could hardly bear it, she's very quick in her movements but rather spoilt. Dear Sarah Short died this evening. Martha Brown and Sarah Giles also died within a few hours of each other. The weather is gloomy and all seems depressed.

Thurs 16th   All was talk of the Bump Supper[38], but we got Charles to invite wives of men as we would have felt awkward to meet all men alone. We took Minnie and Mrs Knibb to Richard Faulkes's, who is the leather cutter living in Milton End. It all looked comfortable and they had good fires going. Old Aunt B.T. arrived in her chair and was ushered in. She took Charles's hand and I rose, but she said, 'We'll waive the usual formality, how do you all do,' then threw off her boa and sat down in first chair inside the door. She made John Winter sit exactly before her to shield her from fire. We all saw she was very cross, perhaps the fete wasn't of her order, came once to the door though wouldn't come in to dinner and said, 'You all look to be enjoying yourselves, plenty of glasses,' She would only have a bit of pudding. Uncle B.T. sat at the head of the table with Mrs Knibb on his left. Charles, self, Kate, Mrs Frise, Hall, Shepherd and Painter to the sperib. Caudle, Francis, Joe, Mr Smith and Mr Frise at two side tables, then the wives and Emma at another. Sam Vines[39] waited at table and later dined with Mrs Faulkes, Painter and daughter and H Greening. We had a fine leg of mutton at head of table, sperib at the foot, potatoes, parsnips, carrots, boiled and baked plum puddings, cheese and celery. We then withdrew and several toasts proposed. They asked for music and Kate and I found 'Beautiful Star' and sang it. Frise bounded in laughing and said, 'More spirit, ladies, play with more spirit and faster.' Emma told me later that Uncle B.T. made fun of our singing. The oldest Painter and Faulkes played and then room was prepared for magic lantern, but we were determined not to enjoy it. The lantern was exhibited much to everyone's delight, especially Tom who laughed excessively and Minnie who laughed too loudly, but I couldn't bring myself to correct her as her grandmother is her immediate charge, but I couldn't help wondering what her father, the Capt would have me do. Ladies then retired while more speeches made and we had wine and cake. Was annoyed that Charles called me out to say that George Clissold had sent note in morning to say he would like bed for the night, and Charles forgot to mention it before. It was most inconvenient, having others here, and he is quite able to afford a bed at the inn, but is very stingy. This is Minnie's birthday. She is 9 years old today.

Mon 20th Frosty and very cold. Spirits very low. I am grieved to see how Charles meets all Minnie's little every request, contrasted to how Kate and I have to beg and beseech him to get anything done, and then often as if irksome, perhaps a frown, often an excuse with a vexed countenance. But if Minnie requests, whether he's reading paper or smoking or whatever, instantly gets every wish attended to with a cheerful smile. Shut myself up alone in my room and began to reason with myself, why should I be so cast down as to envy this little child playing below in the street. I prayed for more tolerance and grace. Snowed heavily, but not, thank goodness, enough to detain George Clissold here longer. Mrs Rice sent me a record of her account of new evangelical college to be built in Huron.

Wed 22nd   Had pig killed yesterday and Anna Frise came to spend time with Minnie. Oh, how wild Minnie was, her noise and hilarity quite drove me to distraction, was relieved when it was their bedtime.

Fri 24th   One wheel very crotchety on coburg on way home yesterday from Cirencester, had to see William Hinks about it myself as Charles said he was too busy. Thought I should have got Minnie to name it to him then he would have jumped up and sped off about it. Emma too in poor mood. I was obliged to make her sweep the dining room again, there was half a dustpan full of dirt. Then she couldn't get the fire to burn. Kate and I salted bacon and were up to our elbows in salt when the Belchers arrived. To add to it all Mr Arkell called to try and induce Charles to pay church rate for Kempsford parish. It is only 1/11d, but he firmly refused.

Sun 26th   Francis had been ordered to be ready for driving us to chapel, but was in bad humour and there was only room for Mrs Knibb and Minnie to ride. Kate and I had to walk to Meysey Hampton in our pattens, it being so wet underfoot. Took Ann Truman some griskin from pig killing.

Mon 27th   Mrs Knibb told Kate yesterday that she heard Capt and I are engaged, but she hasn't named it to me, which I find strange. But I can only think of dear J.

Tues 28th   Policeman brought summons for church rate to Charles. Tom for first time drove us out, went to Furzy Hill. I picked nosegay of yellow jasmine, snowdrops and primroses and evergreen to send to chapel for the farewell tea meeting. Minnie so naughty this morning about going out with us, I had to pick her up from the floor and was going to carry her upstairs to her room to scold her when she suddenly said she would be good and kissed me. She was then good and true to her word. But she tries my patience sorely.

Thurs 30th   Minnie again very tiresome at prayer time. Took her, after her promise to be good, to the Ebenezer Chapel for the wedding. It was full. Gerring and Miss Brown were so amused they kept laughing. Cornelius Cowley married Bess and Mr B and we spoke to them afterwards. Mrs Knibb could not come as her foot was so painful. I bathed it for her and she said, 'I suppose you have heard the report that my son-in-law Captain is going to marry you.' I laughed and said, 'Oh, yes, I have heard, but folks will talk.' Then I spoke to her seriously on the matter and said that I was too anxious a character to bear the separation of seafaring life, and Captain Milbourne was not fitted for business ashore. She said that Minnie made the remark to her yesterday that when they were talking of us taking her to the wedding she said 'I wish Papa would marry Aunt Sarah because I love her so.' I was dumbfounded for she does not show it, though she can be an affectionate loving little thing, her sayings are very amusing, but more often she is just plain tiresome.

Fri 31st I felt anxious about our dear brother, this being the morning for him to appear before the magistrates being summoned for non-payment[40] of church rate for Kempsford parish, but it passed off quietly. Mr Barker, Lord of Fairford Manor, Sir Michael Hicks Beach, the Hon Mr Ponsonby and the Rev Maurice seemed as if they would be glad to let him off, but were obliged to serve him with an order. They said he might as well pay it at once and have done with it, but Charles would not, then Mr Barker said 'Then, Sir, we must distrain upon you.' Charles replied, 'Then, Sir, I must bear it.' Some in court laughed at him, but he returned home in good humour and went later to read about it in paper at the Bull. I feel annoyed with Frise for being too cowardly to go the justice meeting this morning, yet he can prate about it as much as anybody against it when alone. Met Ellen Coles on way back, and she vexed me sorely by saying that the Rev Mr John Davis was at Sheephouse all this week and returned home with her and her cronies after service.

❧ FEBRUARY ☙

Sun 2nd Mrs Knibb's foot rather better but the other is grumbling so I offered to go to Blockley for her as she is anxious that Minnie should go to school. Annie Booker brought us some wedding cake.

Sat 15th I have been unable to continue this till today, having been away from home. Charles drove Minnie and me to Arlington on 4th. Minnie very tiresome again, and left Emma more dead than alive. Mr Cook offered me gig, but went in Spenser's covered cart, Mrs Belcher accompanying me. On reaching Blockley went to Miss Beal's with Minnie where she at once felt at home. We had music in evening, the girls sang and played very nicely and they made me sing Mountain Home. During time away walked up Dovedale. I was enchanted with the spot. A lovely drive running up through thickly planted ground both sides with a wide but shallow stream on the left with a natural waterfall every now and then, quite lovely. On returning saw Miss Beal's school on a lower road. Instantly heard a little voice screaming out, 'I know who it is, it's my Aunty.' It was little Minnie and one of the teachers brought her over to speak to me, she seemed very happy. On another day we were shown some fine marble monuments in church, belonging to Lord Northwick's family and the lately erected Good Samaritan for the late Lord, cost £1,000, most exquisitely executed by a Belgian sculptor[41] in white marble. On the 7th we walked to Packsford. I had a great desire to do so as dear Papa had such an interest in the place. Minnie seemed perfectly happy when I finally left her. Mr Belcher came for us on 8th to drive us home, was most interested in his account of the Act of Conformity when 2,000 good men were expelled from the church, or rather expelled themselves. He stopped at Stow on business. Saw Lord Sezincote's home[42], he was an Indian Nabob. We then called for a short time at Bourton as his sister had met with an accident, being thrown out of gig, her face was quite black and blue. At Sherborne we drove back and fore before we could get on right track and we perished with cold as he would keep stopping to visit several farmers, but fortunate for us, as we shivered waiting for him, the farmers had gone to Faringdon Market. It was 6 before we arrived at their house, then he insisted that Mr Davis should come to practise his singing and we supped while the horses were fed and rested. I felt quite excited but tried not to show it as it is long since we met. He joked and said folks told him he didn't preach so well after he had been to Fairford as his mind was too occupied elsewhere. I was mortified. On arriving home, and after fond greeting from my dear Kitty, Charles brought in Mr Wassell. They had been to Mullens and found that Meysey Hampton chapel belonged to us and not to William and John as we had been led to believe, otherwise the deeds would have to be sent to them in Australia for their signatures. Mrs Knibb so pleased to see me home and have news of little Minnie settling at school, and even Emma delighted to have me back that she can't help saying so. The auspicious day fell on 13th. Charles strove to hide his excitement, though he must have felt it. We reached Meysey Hampton at 5½. Kate and I dressed the females, Susan Lane and Ann Clarke, Martha Ecott and Mrs Kay in front of good fires upstairs.

Then I became anxious about whether our dear brother had changed his dirty socks, as I had entreated him to do so. The baptismal service was very faithful and they all went through it well. Charles looked uncommonly happy. The boards were relaid over the baptistry for there was not another room and all partook of the Lord's Supper. Mr Wassell reminded everyone that we Baptists 'do not go to our neighbours and take their chairs and tables to pay for our bread and wine, we collect for it ourselves and anything over from the donations goes to the poor of the flock'. Emma was so overcome by witnessing it that she is determined to be baptised, but W Hignall has been severe with her about it.

Wed 19th Parted with Mrs Knibb today. Hannah Harris, who arrived unexpectedly yesterday, walked with me to see her off on the coach. Yesterday had converse with Mrs Knibb about Captain Milbourne and told her how our interview occurred. She said she could only wish he was in a position that would enable me to accept him. I told her also of John Davis, but she had heard of it before. I told her that if in London she was questioned about him she might say there was more than friendship between us. Felt relieved that I had thus spoken to her on the matter. Was most annoyed that Mrs Knibb had to go over to say farewell to the Friscs, it is most unkind to the old lady as not once in the seven weeks have they made the effort to come to see her specifically.

Sat 22nd Called on Rose and saw she is such a young sufferer that I thought as I stood by her that I should fear ever to marry, as her illness is owing to first confinement. She cried like a child as she spoke of her pain. I gave her some port wine and endeavoured to cheer her. Cath Mitchell called and tead here, see she still loves dress. Mr Smith came to sup and I paid him a guinea for poor Sarah Short's funeral. Parr came and said that he was at Rices and Mr Rice said he thought 'Mr Kingsley is a great simpleton to spend his money in such a way, there is no great difference between church rates and tithes.' Dear J did not come, though half expected. My eyes turned constantly to corner of shady walk from green door.

Tues 25th Vexed with old Parr having quarrelled with Howse for he does not come now, and all the work standing, says Herbert can do better and he'll see him about doing the pruning.

❧ MARCH ❧

Sun 2nd This would have been dear Papa's birthday. Went to Meysey Hampton and thought much of all his work there, now I have to carry the responsibility of its continuing that which he started. I paid Mr Smith £1 for incidental expenses, but felt vexed that a good fire was kept in the vestry and no one using it. I've remonstrated several times on the waste of money for it, to no avail. Took tapioca pudding to Betty Miller and port wine jelly to Mrs Hewer.

Mon 3rd Had letter from Mrs King to say that Mr would be here today or tomorrow and hopes that he will see Mr Davis. She said she would like to be a mouse in the corner, after all my yeas and nays she shall expect to see an extraordinary nice man. The constable went to Burdocks and said he should come today and fetch sack of barley in payment of church rates, but they haven't been near.

Tues 4th Again no seizure for rates. Mr King came by Collett, then went to dine at Frises. Parr says he can't get a man and 'tis too much for him to do alone, so it all stands while he goes off to do another garden and leaves us in the lurch, yet ours begun long first, two laurels have been out of ground waiting for him, four or five weeks. It all distressed my head so, then Cook came to say he was just going to Burdocks to take the sack of barley. Kate and I reading Tom Brown's Schooldays, wept over Arthur's illness and it made me more humble, but feel very angry and hurt that John doesn't come. Perhaps Providence is answering my prayers in this way and I must first seek the strength to face it, but I fear I rebel, 'tis a strange inconsistency I feel, for I can't help thinking of him day and night, Maria Williams wrote begging for an account of Fairford, the scene of her childhood which is still dear to her memory.

Mon 10th Chatted to Mrs Wakefield in her shop and called on Jane Day. Our new dog arrived, but found him a sore trouble, had it in the parlour.

Tues 11th Charles returned at last by Collett, thankful to hear his business done at last. Mortgage at Maidstone paid off and £300 paid into Cirencester bank. He vexes me sorely at times. I worked hard at mending his coat to the last minute before he left and Kate begged him earnestly to wear it at proper times, putting his new one on if he went visiting. He wore it and hacked it the whole time, not so much as taking the other out of his bag once. Then he pulled a pair of socks out of his bag. He hadn't changed his socks for the whole month because he wouldn't take the trouble to look in his bag. His feet are quite offensive and he didn't once say he was sorry.

Wed 12th Now it is Frise that caused the painful scene. When prayer was named at supper time, he said sharply, 'You can read when I'm gone.' At the same time he seized his pipe and filled it and threw the bible on the table. Kate insisted that reading should be first before Emma went to bed, he said she could go. And this about our servant in our house by a minister. I was mortified to the extreme. I trust he was duly ashamed by our reaction, even Charles was stunned and Emma all of a wonder at it all.

Mon 17th A pouring rain. Went to Meysey Hampton and had quite a turn to find John there, when we passed a greeting felt need for some fresh air, the chapel was full. I didn't fully enjoy the service, found it rather too exciting and Cath Mitchell went into hysterics, I had her on my arm and put cologne on her face, but she made such a noise Mr Rodway came in quite exhausted and we were obliged to send for some brandy to revive her. Many wept, crying for their sins. I can't but think that some good must result. John returned with us and wanted bed for the night, he said he thought Mr Rodway was a single man and perhaps ... it was 2 o'clock before Charles, Kate, he and I went to bed. John slept in outer room but was full of his usual fun.

Tues 18th Tea meeting at Quenington. Mr Brown put a strong stick in the wheel of our coburg as one of the spokes fell out, and he then bound it up with rope, Mr Rodway fishing to find out if dear J came to visit me, and dear J fished off Emma if Mr Rodway was doing the same. Kate had to sort him out and had strong words with him alone to get to the truth of it. He said folks tried to make out I was 42 or 43 years old. He said he thought they did this because they do not consider the union suitable and try to throw discord between us, partly because they don't want him to leave and think he couldn't stay at Arlington if he married and partly because there would be rivalship, they'd think me above them. He was more like himself though and brought our water jug to our room this morning.

Wed 19th Charles, Kate, Mr Rodway and I went to Cirencester. We called at Mrs Keyworths with some of the pig meat from the pig killed on 14th, took Kate's silk dress for Ellen. Then we went on to

Siddington to Mr Fyles's sale. We bought drawing room carpet 20 x 20 and hearth rug in good order for £5 15s. A pretty stone vase for £1 7s, but was vexed to find its fellow was sold for only £1 3s. Francis wheeled carpet to Keyworth's in barrow, returned to tea. Didn't think it safe to return in coburg as wheel was worse, Collett's carrier cart had gone and Charles tried in vain to get conveyance. Mrs Keyworth insisted Kate and I staid night, Charles and Francis rode horse home between them and took harness.

Sat 22nd   Had to stay over as snow quite deep and no conveyance, but arrived back today by Collett. Had letter from Mrs Knibb to say Capt didn't go so far on his journey as intended and will leave Africa by packet mail in February, she spoke with much pleasure of her visit here.

Wed 26th   Keylock brought our carpet and stone vase back for us. Emma not particular with her dusting and I had to do it after her, I feel she is not too well. Mr Coe drove over here and married last Sunday morning in pouring rain at 8½. There were just Mr Coe, his bride and a female. She was not at all like a bride, dressed all in old dark clothes.

Fri 28th   Very damp and mizzly again. The two Miss Belchers arrived tired and dirty from their walk from Arlington, just as Anna Frise and we had done tea. It was good to see them. We like Ellen best. They talked much of dear J which vexed me. Lizzie said that he had taken her and the cousins from Blockley to Ready Token on Monday and returned through the mud of ploughed fields and farmyards. Lizzie said with emphasis 'I hate him.' She then said that when they were at Mrs W Cole's she joked him about me and said 'Why don't you go to see Miss Thomas now?' She then said he replied, 'Because someone else has stolen her from me.' I could hardly believe what they were saying, and then she added that Mrs Cole advised him to go and see Miss Beal and he started asking many questions about her. I felt so poorly late that night I couldn't sleep and I think I am sinking fast under some complaint.

Mon 31st   Emma not well and went to see Mr Cornwall. He said she should have a month's rest. I had a long talk with her and she said she hardly felt strong enough for the work. When I offered her £9 instead of £8 agreed upon, she said she would rather I had a woman in some-times to help than have her wages raised. I agreed to do so and said I

Fairford Workhouse

would give her another 5/- to make up to a sovereign she will then have in the bank. I agreed that she should go home next week. Frise called and so did Hall, offering Aunt Thomas's pew seat to us, Faulkes's have left and she is to have theirs and we can have hers, but I don't know what the pew rent is so said I would consider.

APRIL

Tues 1st Mr Marshall arrived dripping wet and had to change into a pair of Charles's trousers to go to meeting at Crofts chapel. It was crowded. Afterwards the Christians went into the vestry and prayed for the sinners amongst those left in the chapel. I gave Thomas Hignall dinner and half a crown, but was annoyed when he said that all should remain in the church where they were first called, but I had promised him the half crown some days ago and could not pull back, so trust that God will accept it through Hignall. Kate and I quite done up, then the Howards arrived to stay night, without a word of it beforehand, and not a clean thing in the house. Charles was so late in coming home we feared the worse, but when he arrived he said that by The Magpies[43] a young man in a trap had difficulty in managing his horse as the shafts broke, they had no cord and 'twas so difficult, so Charles rode to the White Hart for help and returned to him before he could proceed home.

Sun 6th   Again wet, water everywhere. Yesterday when fire was hung around with sheets and I busy in back parlour, Mr Gloucester called and sat and hindered over two hours, at last we were downright cross although we had given him wine and cake, still he stuck, waiting for dinner we supposed. He said Mr Roff had told him to call to see how we were. Well Roff only lives in the same street and I didn't care if he thought me rude by saying so.

Tues 8th   Francis drove Kate and me to Cirencester this being the anniversary service and tea meeting. Chapel full. John and Mrs Belcher walked from Arlington late, wanted to come back with us though trap was full as we had promised to bring Frise home, but then he made us feel awkward as he said he would walk to Sheephouse to sleep so we had to squeeze in. Neither Frise nor John passed a word with us behind until we nearly home. At last Kate asked John to change seat, it was uncouth of them not to notice we hadn't room. John has bad cold and is out of sorts, we gave him water for his feet and warmed his bed which he much liked. About 2 our door opened and we thought it was robbers, but 'twas Charles looking for brandy as he was shivering and not well. I gave him our bottle for his feet, more warm clothing, a night light and tucked him up with strict instructions he was to call if he couldn't sleep, but naughty boy, he broke his promise and soon after was sick so I wrote a note to Mr Cornwall and he sent him some medicine.

Wed 9th   John came to our room for brush and comb. He has been quite dull and stupid like with his cold all day. He left at 7 having perversely refused wine or brandy and 'tis so cold for his walk home. Emma is home and we are our own mistresses and maids. I felt John was not very affectionate when we were in the kitchen and if so he won't do for me. I don't feel quite pleased with him now.

Thurs 10th   A pouring wet day. Uncle B.T. lectured at Meysey Hampton on 'The Constitution of Man'. He had Collett's large van and our two horses to take schoolchildren from here to sing at intervals during the lecture while he rested. The horse kicked and all were obliged to get out at Waiten Hill and get our waggon instead of van. Charles took some of them in Brown's trap. The chapel was full, but the folk don't like to be displaced for the children and some are annoyed.

Fri 11th   Can get neither Mrs Rose or Wall. Just sat down to dinner when Mr Bullock walked in but he took it all in the rough that we didn't mind him a bit. In the evening we played double chess. Mr Bullock and I beat Charles and Kate.

Sat 12th Mrs Wall came for a few hours. Went to asylum for Dorcas subscription. She gave Kate two nitre balls for her throat, told us her son Richard had got into trouble breaking windows and the policeman came for him and everyone knows about it. When we returned found Aunt B.T. in parlour, she was unusually agreeable.

Thurs 17th Sarah Wassell came on Tuesday, couldn't feel very glad to see her. She and Mr Bullock played chess all next morning and didn't even take clothes off her bed or offer to help us. She showed off about music but wouldn't play although requested. Walked to Meysey Hampton today and I took the sick their eggs and money such as we could afford and Ma's old boa to Ann Truman. Charles gave a lecture on the Bicentenary of 1662, the first time he has spoken in public. The chapel was full though folks were busy gardening, he was rather nervous but acquitted himself well. Later, Sarah and I had a long talk over each other's failings, we spoke plainly and coolly, but I had best of it.

Good Friday Sarah again tiresome. She got in a temper over going to chapel and bounced off upstairs and threw herself on the bed. I had had enough of her and told her I was sick and tired of her conduct. She was in a great rage. I told her we had never had such a visitor as her and I had never been treated so badly as when I visited them. Then Charles was late in again and had staid to smoke, though we had asked him to be home early. We might as well entreat the stones, yet we do everything to please him.

Wed 23rd Have had another night of wakefulness and suffering, could not lie down in bed for pain in chest and spat up blood twice. Kate sent for Mr Cornwall in morning, he said I was very poorly. Mr Ferris visited and staid overnight. He was very chatty and agreeable, but did not take enough notice of Sarah for her to like him, so she said he was a sawney. Had parcel from Arlington. John sent wrapper and wrote kind note saying he was sorry that he was not able to come as intended, but Lea's folk were all coming to Albert's wedding and there wouldn't be room for him to ride with them, and he must be home early to marry them. I was pleased to hear from him, resisted the temptation to write to him in return.

Fri 25th   Mr Cornwall called again, though I am feeling somewhat recovered, especially as Sarah has made herself so agreeable since our quarrel. We have, in consequence, asked her to stay till Wednesday and she seemed delighted. I want her to see dear J and yet don't want her there with him. Kate warned her in strong terms against making Mrs Dyer her bosom friend, but Sarah thinks highly of her which is more than we do.

Tues 29th   A day of visitors: Mrs Keyworth and Jones were driven by Brassington here in the morning, then Mrs King and Sarah Stephens were announced early afternoon, followed by dear J. I was taken by surprise and felt rather stiff and formal, and thought him cool in return, it rather depressed me, silly thing, especially as I saw he could be free with Sarah Wassell. I blamed myself for failing to reply to his letter of last week. He didn't seem to care about staying the night as we had so many here, but he did. Belchers came early evening and we played with the dogs on the lawn as John brought them out to join us, then he and Sarah Wassell sang after supper, which is exactly as I anticipated would happen if they met. When she and I and Mrs King were alone later, she said if John had made an offer to her she should have him. Mrs King said, 'He's a very nice man, dear, and tis very wicked of you to say No, Sarah.' This was sweet to me and when I looked on him as he said Goodnight to me, I couldn't help feeling a little proud of him but I tried to keep him at a distance.

Wed 30th   Sarah Wassell left by Collett's carrier cart. Kate says dear J is anxious to know what is the matter with me and said he had prayed for me, this found favour in my eyes but I still feel we are at cool corners. I am looking at papers for our room, and after Kate and I had chosen, I asked dear J to name the one he liked, and lo and behold, without knowing my choice, he pointed to the very one out of the two large books of patterns. After dinner John laid on sofa and Tom King, who had arrived in morn, laid by fire. I watched dear J's face as he dozed. My heart yearned for him and after, when Tom had gone out, he made me sit with him on the little sofa and asked me what was the trouble. For a long time I protested that all was well, then emotions overtook me and I admitted he wounded me by his constant flirtations, harmless though he says they are. He seemed surprised that I should be wounded by his sending his love to Emily when we go to Weymouth and playfully suggested that he should take her with him to Columbia. He said he had no idea I loved him enough to care and I tried to say I didn't. I am too proud to let him know just how much I do love him. We had a long time together and when we finished he kissed me and begged for some bread and cheese. After he had packed it in his pocket to eat on the way home he ran upstairs and later called out for me to go to him as he needed sticking plaster having cut his chin. I walked in garden with him, then Kate came looking for us and she walked with him to the green door. I watched them cross the lawn and linger for some time at the green door, my mind was too full of other things to act normally at our parting, for much else passed than I can note, and I wept. Again he pressed me to say a final Yes, and again I could not. Then he said, 'You had better remain an old maid, and I an old batchelor.' I said, 'I won't. No. You've spoilt me for that.'

MAY

Fri 2nd Dear Kate and I chatted ourselves to sleep over John's visit, I tried to cast my cares on the Lord, feeling so low. Was in poor mood to have visitors, Mrs Frise and Harriet to tea. Susan Cornwall came as we were clearing, but staid for fresh pot. She too is very low. Her Ma is poorly so I sent her one of the pigeons Mrs Hewer sent us. Says her Ma and Pa have much trouble with young Charles Cornwall, he stays out very late, and her Ma feels it sadly, she sits and cries over his ways.

Mon 5th A lovely summer's day. Mrs King came to my room to chat while I dressed. I confided in her about dear J and said my objections to him as I thought she liked him much and by this means thought she would help to influence my mind towards accepting him, so was most pained to find she spoke so differently to what she did last week when Sarah Wassell was here. She said she feared he was not well educated enough for me, that I should perhaps sometimes feel a little ashamed that I couldn't look up to him and that he would never look up to me, as that is in his nature. She said he is very amiable and most likeable, but not intellectual enough, and that to accept hand in marriage it must be without any ifs and buts. Had much on my mind as we cleared our two bedrooms for whitewashing and papering tomorrow. Kate went to old Parr after much deliberation as he hasn't been for months. They had quite a set to. He at first being very haughty then quite ashamed and turned up and put dahlias in. Kate had told me every syllable of their conversation and I was ready to say 'O fie, couldn't have thought it Mr Parr,' but all I said was 'Now don't be so silly next time.' He said the garden was looking very nice and did us credit.

Thurs 8th   Mrs King and Kate called on Uncle and Aunt B.T. I had much vexation with work people. The paper not come right and the painters put wrong colour on, made Beale alter it, which he didn't much like. Neither Mrs Wall nor Mrs Rose could come, stops everything.

Fri 9th   Mrs King spent day with Mrs Frise as so much to do over painters here. I sent a dish of asparagus which I cooked to the Frises as Mrs King dined there and I wanted to be sure she had something worthwhile. Poor Harriet called this morning, she has a nasty cough, which I fear could end in decline. She is going back with Mrs King. Frank brought nice bit of pudding for me and asked to go round garden, naughty boy, he turned the vase over on the lawn and might have injured himself. Mrs Cornwall sent a nice piece of eel. Mrs Crew came to alter the carpet, a most troublesome affair.

Sat 10th   Got rid of painters, paperers and whitewashers today. I had a serious talk with one of the painters, he seemed quite Christian and I gave him tracts and lent him copy of Weaver's Life. Mrs King, Kate and I went to Miss Truman's showroom, while we were out Jane Iles had called. After tea, Elizabeth Iles, Miss Tanner, whom I had not met before but was quite pleased with our first interview, joined us for a walk round gardens where I had never been before. The gardener said it was after time, but after gentle coaxing he allowed us round as Elizabeth said she was a friend of Mrs Powell's (the Roman Catholic).

Mon 12th   Oh, what a trying day this has been. Tried deeply and severely in various ways, though trifling in themselves seem more hard to bear patiently at the time than heavier ones. First, Mrs Rose was engaged to come today to do the wash and then arrived, begging to be let off as Mrs Lea wants her. I pointed out that ours was the prior engagement, but she was afraid to tell Mrs Lea so I sent Emma with a note, but Mrs Lea turned funny about it and said she employed her more frequently than we did, so we had better get someone else. After much toing and froing we got Mrs Rowland to come and she was delighted to be asked but the time had got on to start the wash. Visited the Savory's, saw Lucy and babe, Ellen Coles and Sam besides others. Mrs King vexed when we returned at Kate saying they all seemed so worldly. No John, felt disappointed as I expected him but feared last meeting was not ended so satisfactorily, then Mrs King went into hysterics as she had a letter from Mrs Stephens to say her brother is not so well. I was glad to bury my cares and sorrows in sleep.

Fairford Market Place

Wed 14th   Fair Day. Our new woman got through the heavy wash and the clothes dried nicely. We like her as yet, though 'tis early to judge. Happily no visitors after Mrs King left by Colletts, although the Hewers had said they might come and she would have staid here while he went to the Fair. Pleased they didn't, spent the day starching two bed furniture, frocks and skirts in abundance, besides the fine things. My hands are almost raw.

Thurs 15th   I went to Cirencester by Collett. Called at Miss Bury's and dined at Keyworths. Bought little money box with which I am delighted as I shall keep it for Our Lord's Treasury, and put in it offerings for Him when I remember how much we owe to Him. Saw baptising gown at Keyworths and Mrs said that dear J was there baptising on Tuesday and left yesterday. That explained why he did not come to Fairford and removed all uncomfortable feelings for his absence.

Thurs 22nd   Weymouth: the last day or two before we left was almost harrassed to death, gardening and finishing ironing and the newly done rooms. Kate went to fetch Hannah from Arlington on Friday in coburg, we brought it home the night before. It looks nice but the bill is £8. Kate said John had tead with her at Belchers and had asked kindly after me. He said I must get out in the air more and get more appetite. He told Kate that he might run down here to Weymouth while we are here if there is an excursion train. On Saturday I called on Mrs Rice and gave her 17/6d for the New Evangelical College being erected in America. Then went to see Mrs Reynolds's things for the bazaar, we were struck to see such a large collection and we took a few articles as well. Charles had returned from London so we all went to Meysey Hampton and I took 1/- to Betty Miller, saw Martha Ecott's husband and offered him a tract but he said he couldn't read. He was very bluff. As I walked home with Hannah she spoke of baptising at Arlington and of a chapel member who was dismissed for improper conduct with a man in a barn, she said how they all thought it was difficult for Mr Davis being a single man to deal with such matters and all wished he was married. Then she said how he was always fondling Ellen Belcher and kissing her and squeezing her hand, and that when they all went on the long walk, he took her off, leaving Hannah, Lizzy and M Belcher behind tired out and Lizzy so faint she was obliged to sit down. Hannah got quite warm when she was telling me these things. She said Ellen made out she disliked him all the time, but it was a shame of him and he'd be sure to go on till he got himself and others into trouble. She said too that he would go to Leas's and stay there will 12 at night or 1 in the morning. I was grieved and mortified. I went to bed with a heavy heart and determined never to think anything more of him. So busy preparing for our journey had no time to share my troubles with dear Kate. Then dear Mr Cornwall called and poor man, seemed so poorly. He talked of running away before we returned. I was so distressed to hear our old family doctor talk thus, it made me very low, but he said he would tell us if he did go.

Tuesday was a day of worry, couldn't get train bill, then old Parr came and bothered us, supped and sat till after 12 teazing about Charles going to Barker at the Park about Giles's house to settle his life on it. Emma was in bad temper and Hannah became very dull. When we got to Cirencester and Charles took us to station the master said he couldn't give us second class tickets for Weymouth, so we staid night at Keyworths and went third class just from Swindon to Chippenham, but second each journey to there and beyond, paid 9/1d each. Mrs Keyworth said that Mrs King and Mrs Mountain had both said how much they liked Mr Davis, and the latter said he was certainly very superior. Thus, in numberless cases I have two influences constantly working on me, for and against him. Kate said I must only take half of what Hannah had told me, as some would be told in disappointment and spite because he did not look to her.

Sat 24th We received kind welcome from all when we arrived. Dear Emily looked ill and Gertrude sadly old, she keeps much aloof from everyone, she breakfasts in bed and sups in kitchen and is a great trial to all. We called on Mr and Mrs Ellis, she is a sweet woman, he rather fast. We took bread and cheese and walked to Sandsfoot Castle and ate our meal on the beach. We were annoyed to see Union boys treat the little ones so roughly in the water. Returned at 4½ very very tired.

Thurs 29th   Mrs Davis, Gertrude, Kate and I went for lovely walk although Gertrude made a fuss about it, we were ferried on a little boat, then a heavy thunderstorm came on and we had to take off our crinolines and laughed at our straitened circumstances determined it should not spoil the day.

Fri 30th   Dr Brown called this morning and spoke harshly to Gertrude, said she should leave home whether or no, she cried sadly and upset us all, then flew off to school. Had packet from home. Charles cannot come this week and Ellen Booker wrote to give description of the folks wanting our house and needing more particulars.

❧ JUNE ❧

Sun 1st   The day began sadly. Emily poorly and Kate not well. Gertrude said her Ma had been telling her Aunt Eliza about her and she fumed sadly. Mrs Davis was upset because we were to dine at Birts. Gertrude is very queer, but went with us for a walk to the cemetery in evening, we much enjoyed it and delighted to see green hedges again.

Tues 3rd   Mr and Mrs Birt came to tea. When Gertrude came into room she looked as black as thunder. Mrs Birt rose and went to her saying, 'Well, Gertrude, dear, how are you?' offering to kiss her. Gertrude turned away abruptly keeping her at arm's length. Mrs Birt was quite overcome and I feared would go into hysterics but overcame it for the moment and had it afterwards upstairs. Mr Birt was most kind throughout supper though Gertrude spoke not one syllable to any one of us. She sat in the only low chair, there being no other. Kate and I sang several songs in the evening in an attempt to make it enjoyable. Since we have been here, poor Kate and I have suffered much from costiveness. Went into the closet and was there nearly an hour in much pain never have I been so.

Thurs 5th   Kate and I had just gone upstairs to dress for dinner when Emily came to hurry us, on coming down found dear Charles had arrived. Most vexed to hear that about 20 cows had got into our garden and did immense mischief. It seems Mrs Barrett had called and

Emma opened the garden door to show her the view of the church across the Green and had not bolted it securely.

Sat 7th   Charles, Kate and I had long walk after we had bathed. Took him to see Mr Stafford's house and Charles asked after apartments to let, having seen paper up. We were shown round, terms for four rooms 25/- a week. Kate and I had letter from Kidd, he sent Kate his likeness again, and wants to visit Fairford.

Mon 9th   A fine day. Mrs Davis, Charles, Kate and I started at 8½ and had a lovely sail, then had carriage to Pensylvania Castle and paid 3/- for us all. There we were charmed by the rich foliage of the trees in the midst of so barren a spot, it was most striking. There we had our sandwiches and went to see landslip, caught in a storm and hurried back to summer house, took slips and cuttings to take home for Emily. Having dismissed the carriage we walked to quarry and saw the caverns and bore off part of them. We then went to Breakwater Hotel. Charles ordered two glasses of brandy and water of which we partook and refreshed ourselves nicely. Mrs Davis was very worn out and returned by 4 o'clock boat and we trudged on weary and footsore to breakwater. We returned by boat and dear Lily had provided a very refreshing tea for us.

Tues 10th   Ellen Booker wrote to say the folks thought the terms unusually high for our house. Mary came with us to Upway. We had waited to ride on the waggon which was to be by St John's Church, but it was filled and went on unheeding our perplexity. Then we met Miss Styfield and she saw two little boys with donkeys and she sent them back for donkey carriage but then we spied a waggon, low and empty except for two men, one woman and the driver. He consented to take us and the labourers got out to walk to make room for us. The woman was a great oddity, she prated fast and merrily and when she got out ran alongside the waggon holding Charles's hands and saying she longed to see him again. Charles gave the man 1/- for driving us and a 1/- between the two men. When we returned we wrote to Ellen Booker to say we would take a guinea a week, and they must find all linen and plate.

Thurs 12th   Charles left for Brockenhurst to meet Mr Forbes, to go with him to Lymington and thence to Totton. Emily had long confab last night with Charles about the evils of smoking.

Sat 14th Heard from Ellen to say that Sharples had declined to take our house. Went to dentist in evening, Kate had one stopped. Wind very rough, waves dashed over esplanade, Mrs Davis quite feared for us as the window was blown out of omnibus in which Jessie came home last night from school.

Mon 16th Was racked with toothache and had no sleep. Went to Mr Baker's with Kate and Jessie, he gave me a lovely nosegay with firefly verbena in it. He said, 'You are fond of flowers and I like to give them to people who appreciate them.' He was most kind and sent his little niece to gather us strawberries and gave us sugar to eat with them. It was a very large plate and said that if we didn't eat them all he would think we did not like them. When he had left us a moment I put eight of the largest in my pockets to take back for Mrs Davis and Lily.

Tues 17th In much pain with my tooth which is now so elongated I couldn't shut my mouth, then Emily upset me by saying I could eat more of the sole which I left on my plate though I was in great pain. Mrs Davis, kind as ever, made me sops. Kate brought me tincture to rub on gum to relieve the pain. We're all working hard to get Gertrude's clothes ready. Her Ma has been trying to get her to look them out for wash or to give up her keys. She asked Kate and I to talk to her as she thinks we have good influence over her, eventually we persuaded her to sort them, now 'tis a great hurly burly. Wrote yesterday to Mrs Knibb replying to her letter about Minnie coming. Poor Captain Milbourne is six weeks overdue and no tidings. We fear for him.

Fri 20th I felt almost faint as Mr Baker did my tooth for stopping, he kindly gave me a cordial draught. He told Kate and me yesterday that he has separated from his wife for two years now, she had such a temper that it was impossible to live with her, so they took a child each. He calls his little one his little pet and spoke so nicely of his afflictions. Heard from Mrs Knibb, Capt off Liverpool, is expected in London daily. She says he will bring Minnie to Fairford. It gives me much anxiety. Emily will keep talking about Mr Davis and the Capt, she still begs me to have dear J and says I should excuse away his foibles. Last night went with Emily and Kate to Royal Hotel to hear Christy's Minstrels, enjoyed some of it greatly, but found some parts very low and coarse. The noise at the commencement sent dear Kate into hysterical fit of laughing and crying, but she soon overcame it. I was amazed at Mr Christian's wonderful compass of voice, he sang the

Tyrolean Air. Tonight went to hear Maquire's lecture on Papal agression, or something of the sort. It has been all confusion, glad the last day has come.

Sat 21st   Heard from Charles that Mr Forbes, whom he likes much, and boy return with him to Fairford. The boy to remain for his health. Had to write to postpone it as Milbourne is coming. I was quite upset at having to do it and tried to make it a polite note, but had told Charles we couldn't have them till July. Mary and Gertrude left this morning, and right glad we are to have the bustle over, it was unbearable.

Mon 23rd   Rose early to pack and have last dip. Dined early and called on Mr Baker, he told us more of his domestic history and gave me another lovely nosegay. Mrs Davis, unknown to us, sent for carriage at 3½ and we all rode to Pebble Beach, enjoyed it amazingly, it was a lovely afternoon, met the Birts and they pressed us to take tea. Mr Birt and I had long chat about the High Calvinists, he called the rank ones greasy and double tongued. As we've been prevented from seeing the old suffering woman, gave 2/6d to Ann to give her, I had already asked God to accept it so couldn't draw back. We were both upset by letter from Charles saying it couldn't be helped now and Mr Forbes must come. I had to write to Mrs Knibb and put her off. It has amazingly put us out and vexes Kate and me with Charles's want of consideration and Mr Forbes's ungentlemanly persistency, though urged by Charles.

Tues 24th   Travelled home, all very kind, provided us with eatables and wine for the journey. A curate travelled with us from Maiden Newton to Swindon, a most worthy Christian, we told him we were dissenters and he spoke most nicely about difference of sects in religion. Francis met us with coburg at Cirencester and we stopped to buy 1½ dozen straw dinner mats. Tead at Keyworths and found all when we got back to Fairford quite well. Hannah seemed better though not strong. Charles had letter from Capt, we opened it and laughed as Capt begged Charles to accept a grey parrot for us which he brought from Africa. We thought the garden and house looked so nice and felt very pleased to return once more.

Wed 25th   Spent the day unpacking and writing letters.

Fri 27th   Charles and Forbes came at 10 on Wednesday. Charles quite quiet as he's suffering a little from hay fever, took Forbes to see the church. Ellen Booker called and told us all about Sharples and we are glad now they will not be coming to take the house. Forbes walked round the garden with me and had long talk over Ben and Charles, wants to separate their connection and for us all to go elsewhere to live. I referred to the letter postponing his visit saying that it had been arranged for him to come in July as others were coming this month and we could not have all together as our servant was not strong and it threw much upon ourselves and our own health was not equal to it. I said that our friends were obliged to take the little girl from school to lodgings and he made not the least apology which made me the more angry.

Sun 29th Forbes left yesterday by coach, leaving his boy behind, whom we like much the best of the two. Kate and I called on the Cornwalls. Susan said she had something to communicate to us but would come up here to do it. Charles had letter from Capt and sent many loving expressions in it which annoyed me. I don't want him and I see what he'll be up to again. Charles went to morning school at Meysey Hampton, all went over the way to chapel in the evening, except for Fred Forbes who went to the Crofts Chapel.

Mon 30th Had letter from Mr East and from Emily. Hannah is most helpful, helped us deck out the back parlour. My spirits are much depressed. My thoughts will still go after dear J. Felt vexed that he had written note to Frise asking him to let Miss Thomas have six tickets for Arlington tea meeting, 'tis stupid I know and I have to spend time in prayer, oh, cold and sinful that I am, what should I do without this resort. I cannot understand myself. My thoughts are full of John now that I'm returned home and I feel I love him more than anyone else. I don't want to see

Capt, yet I'm not prepared to accept Mr Davis and fear were he to come again I should do just the same as before. May God help me out of this distressing state. I feel disgusted with John when I hear of his foolishness with the girls, yet I feel I love him deeply.

❦ JULY ❧

Wed 2nd   Charles is so glum that it distresses me. He never speaks at meals and reads all through breakfast, he only spoke normally and chattily when Mr Smith came and went back to his silence when he departed, bringing remarks from Fred Forbes about it. Kate went up to Charles's room and asked what was the matter, he said he was distressed about my letter asking him to put Forbes off and he has so many things on his mind he cannot sleep or shake them off.

Fri 4th   Charles received letter from Capt again, this time enclosing one for me asking me to go to town on Monday and see Mrs Knibb before she sails to return to Jamaica. He added that he wishes to chat to me *on matters of considerable importance*. In Charles's he speaks of his connection with the African Aid Society, still thinking of going there, so it seems to make my way clear and sets my mind at ease. Dear J is always in my thoughts while I seldom think of Captain, but I believe John cares nothing for me and can't help thinking he is not the one for me. It vexed us that Mrs Knibb could not come down here again and roused our anger more against Forbes. Charles and I wrote to Capt saying I had scalded my foot last night and could not get my shoe on so couldn't come to town, I expressed much regret at not seeing Mrs Knibb and wrote to her too.

Mon 7th   To my amazement as I left back kitchen to join Kate in garden, I saw a hat over the wall and someone just opening the gate, which turned me all over, as the next moment brought me hand to hand with Mr Davis, but I iced all over at first. He preached at Cirencester yesterday, rode Purnell's pony and rode it here today. He joined us in garden, friendly but a little cool until we sat together on the sofa in front parlour, then warmed up and soon he was as he used to be. We sang and played music after tea and showed him our newly papered rooms. After early supper he rode home.

Tues 8th   Felt in sad indecision about going to Arlington tea meeting, after much persuasion agreed to go, Frise came with us and we took Fred much to his delight. I was much vexed by Mr Smith leaning over the form and saying aloud, 'Miss Thomas, we've a long bill against you. Did you keep Mr Davis at Fairford last evening, he ought to have been at the meeting.' Before I could reply someone took his attention, and though 'twas said good humouredly, I was upset. Then Ed Lock introduced himself, so grown I hardly knew him. Mr and Mrs Rodway very pleased to see us, he's coming to Kempsford in August, he spoke very nicely. Mr Davis seemed quiet and thoughtful, indeed a serious note pervaded the evening. We supped at Belchers and dear J walked down to sup there with us and the day passed better than I expected, but my mind is more at ease having seen him and felt his renewed kindness. I am like a cat at a mouse, sure of her prey she's happy and content to watch its rambles, directly it gets too far she fears losing it, she feels anxious and concerned. I am shamed of myself and pray to God to give me decision and direction.

Wed 9th Took Fred with us to Cirencester in coburg but rain prevented us going into park to eat our sandwiches so had them in coburg. Later tead at Keyworths, she was quite startled when I told her Captain Milbourne was coming and she feared he would be seeking my hand as she likes dear J much. Bought window curtains at Bowlys for 16/9d.

Fri 11th Fred Forbes went down to ask Susan Cornwall to tea but she had company. Frank came to play with him instead, poor fellow, he is low at leaving us tomorrow. He asked many questions about dear Papa's work at Meysey Hampton and when we told him that all the expenses rested on us he persisted in making me take 1/- towards it, then afterwards added another florin. I resisted in vain as he said it would give him pleasure in giving to good things and that is how he had been brought up. Poor little fellow, his heart is full up having to leave us. We shall miss him.

Sat 12th Charles went to Cirencester to collect Capt and Minnie, they arrived about 8 o'clock. I was about 10 minutes before coming down and felt under restraint but he met me with much warmth and had brought two parrots, one for us and one for Minnie. He looked much as usual and I could but admire him, though I did not show it.

Mon 14th Capt asked us to choose a likeness of himself and Mrs Knibb and Minnie in a group and another just of himself. He sent Minnie for a walk with the Frise children, then took my arm in garden and said, 'Well, Sarah, dear, I have come to claim you and I can take no denial.' We then went into front parlour at his request and he told his plans in regard to Africa. My heart failed me to give the decided Nay and I listened, but said little and felt very sorrowful. Then he proposed we should kneel down and seek direction from above and he prayed with great earnestness and simplicity that it seemed to warm my heart and he gave me a few days to think it over. But I felt I should be obliged to decline, though I agreed to think it over. Very busy the rest of the day picking fruit for preserving.

Tues 15th   The weather very threatening. Started at 9½ for Woodhouse. It was a grand day in Cirencester with Oddfellows and we saw their procession, the rest of the party had gone on so we soon followed and had to go to the second gate before we could enter the park on account of the archery. We lost our way but had a pretty secluded ride and came in at the back of the Woodhouse. Our party was made up of the Belchers and Keyworths, Lizzie from Blockley, Alice and Ellen, Eunice Harris, Polly and Ed Baker, Ed Locke, Miss Barrett, Ruth Smylie, Orlando and Boswell, with Charles, Kate, self, Minnie and Capt and Francis. Mr Davis was obliged to attend meeting of Primitives at Winson sorely against his will, but much to my relief. Some of the party walked blindfolded to the sundial and some fell over Mr Keyworth who laid down in front of them for fun. Then we played Teazel and all much enjoyed it. We walked to Ten Ridings and sang several hymns. When we left saw fire balloon ascend and burst. Thousands streamed from the gate by turnpike to Market Place and we were glad to get home safely. The day was spoiled for me by Alice saying that she thought Mr Davis was so light and trifling, so unlike the Capt, and he would probably be pleased if I accepted the Capt as he would soon get someone else, if he hadn't already. I said it matters not what anyone said, I had full proof that his attachment to me was quite sincere, but I felt it deeply.

Sat 19th   My scalded foot suffered for the day's pleasure and was much swollen. Busy picking fruit last two days. We all went to tea at Belchers as they invited Capt over with us, Mrs Cook, Ruth Smylie, Alice and Ellen there and we tead in summer house. John came before we finished tea and started playing with Ellen and snatched her hand-kerchief, but when we dispersed round the garden he followed me at a distance. I felt extremely awkward and tried to keep away from both. Capt asked me this morning to give a final Yes, but I begged off till tomorrow. After tea we all weighed: John 1.0.15; Kate and self 1.0.32, then Capt and Charles both the same. John had to go to prayer meeting and Capt tried hard for us to leave before he returned, but Bessie Coles, three Bartons and Charlotte Belcher came in and we sat chatting and then had music and songs, Locke sang two comic songs. When John returned he sang with Kate and me The Swallows, but I felt my voice failing me as I was so agitated, then he asked Capt if he would take him to Africa, and Capt declined which tickled us both. John walked with us to coburg then walked off. Capt very quiet all the way home, I felt I needed comforting, but he was so quiet and reserved. Emma poorly so sent her to bed, and we sat round kitchen fire talking a while.

Sun 20th Dear Kate and I had but three hours' sleep for we laid talking so long. Kate and Minnie went to chapel and Capt seeing me unprepared, said he would stay too. He took me in front parlour and asked me again for decision. Though I intended to say No, it wasn't so. He sat me on his knee and said he would have to say Yes for me. I said I wasn't prepared to say No and yet I didn't say Yes. He was most kind and gentle and again proposed prayer. This won me most of all, I couldn't help feeling that if dear J had ever done the same, matters would have been very different. I felt that as he had sought heavenly guidance this gave me confidence. He then claimed me as his own and said he should ever consider me such. None of it seemed of my doing and I thought back to the winter evening when all drew lots for me between the Capt and John, and all drew the Capt. I felt a higher hand was in it and I was being drawn almost against my will. Dear Kitty felt it deeply when I told her and my heart bled for her. I felt the calm had been ruffled and I shivered with excitement for I can't yet feel at ease over it.

Wed 23rd My mind in a turmoil, I cannot get dear J out of my thoughts. Very busy and tired so didn't go to children's treat yesterday, then today Mrs Frise ran over to see if Kate was ready to go to tea meeting at Poulton, I busy preserving. She offered to take the small tray of jams and jellies into parlour and upset it all down her dress and on kitchen stones. I decided not to go to Poulton as it was announced that Mr Davis would be there so I didn't go, but he was not. Heard from the Wassells that Sarah's wedding is quite set aside and we feel much for them as it must be a great mortification.

Sat 26th Capt wrote to Charles seeking my hand, he wants to marry me at once and he'll come to talk it over. I wrote immediately to decline. Ed Locke is becoming a nuisance, he wants Capt to take him, and he came professing to talk to Charles about it. We were tired to death but he would stay tea, then Morty Stephens walked in from Cirencester, so he had to tea here too.

Sun 27th Visitors all day and my mind so heavy and depressed, so occupied by Capt's proposal. The separation when he is in Africa seems so very formidable that I don't think I could face it, but he is evidently fearful of leaving me behind untied, but I can't do it up in a hurry. Though I suppose on some accounts it might be better rather than all this indecision, but the responsibility of training Minnie presses on me also.

Tues 29th   Francis called at Arlington on his way back from Cirencester on Sunday and brought Alice and Ellen over. They said that Mr Davis felt the Capt being here with me, all noticed it. I feel I cannot get my heart back from him, I like to hear of him. The day for laying the foundation stone of Independent Chapel here. Kate had forgotten and so Havers arrived, but went on to ram sale, then returned with Fyfield to smoke with Charles in evening, Mrs Wall came and cooked leg of mutton for supper as we expected folks from Arlington, but they didn't come. Felt disappointed though I take it to be the hand of Providence. Went to bazaar in afternoon, things very poor, only bought antimacasser for 5/-. Capt wrote urging me to have matter over at once, that I must reconsider. Spoke to Charles about it briefly, then we decided not to think of it and I wrote to Capt to that effect and Charles posted it, he can't bear to think of my going to Africa if I marry Capt now.

Wed 30th   Alice and I went to bazaar and spent 10/- on rubbish. Met Ed Locke he badly wants to go to Africa with Capt, he came and supped then we had music. Secretly hoped that Capt would come back by coach, though I had put him off, as he made it hinge on my consent to marry him at once, in that case he'd come to talk over details.

Thurs 31st   Mr Cornwall came to see Kate, she has had much pain in her bowels again and her arm is troublesome. I not at all well either. Mr Bullock rode in to dinner, then we went to Meysey Hampton though I felt too sadly to do much for those whose souls should be seen to. Had brandy and sugar at Mrs Hewer's and rested a little before going to chapel. A goodly number baptised and went through it well, there was a great crowd and they would stand up on seats and broke a window. I gave James Mitchell 1/6d as he had to lose half day's work to be baptised. Charles met Mr Wassell and Alice in the coburg at Cirencester so Kate and I rode Mr Bullock's pony in turns to return home.

⚓AUGUST⚓

Fri 1st   Mr Wassell most anxious to know how Capt had fared this time. He didn't seem to like it at first, said I should always have to maintain him and I should lead an anxious life, but if I accept him I ought to consent to marry at once and most likely Capt would write and ask me to reconsider the thing, and I ought to comply. I felt it had a painful effect upon my mind, which is too easily swayed by opinions of others. Difficulties loomed large in front of me and I could only see a life ahead of unrest and care. In evening walked to Burdocks after gardening. Mr Locke joined us, it made me cross for he was unasked.

Tues 5th   Last evening wrote to Capt and said I would consent but can't fully decide until I've seen him again. I conferred about it first to Charles and dear Kitty and they both thought it was destined to be the right step, but my mind is still uneasy and I trust it will all be set aside. I have a secret feeling that God is guiding me and I dare not doubt His word. Visited Mrs Hewer, Charles caught us up at The Magpies so we rode rest of the way in the van as he had hired Collett to take things over to the chapel. Wrote to tell Mrs Howard and invited Cecily and Kate to be bridesmaids if I finally decide on it. Strolled over the fields with the Hewers and found exquisite little white moth which I carried to the house. Got Alice to send it to dear J as though from herself, but she would not and despite my entreaties, said I had caught it for him. I then found myself telling her the reason. I showed her the ring on my finger and said 'This is a pledge from another.' She was surprised then laughed to see how grave I looked and said I looked as though I had received my death warrant rather than a marriage proposal. She said she was glad it was the Capt and not Mr Davis, but I couldn't help feeling hurt that others speak slightly of him, even now.

Wed 6th   Had letter from Capt. Poor fellow seems in low spirits, wonders why I've not written, and hopes 'tis all right. He said perhaps he had been too pushing and he would yield to my wishes, but my affirmative has reached him ere this. Dear Alice chatted halfway through the night to me about it all, she is so rejoiced and spoke so lovingly of him that it was soothing to me. I read part of Capt's letter to her and she thought it was beautiful.

Thurs 7th   Called on Mrs Lytton, then on Ecott and gave trousers for the son, gave 1/- to Ann Clark for her mother, waistcoats to Norton and Clark, and three shifts to Snelling. Had our first drive in the phaeton, then it rained but drew into stalls until it ceased then drove to Ready Token, Betty's Grave and round by Poulton. Everyone remarks that I look suddenly two years younger, and I must admit my heart seems lighter. Dear Alice I love her much and I feel she will be a great comfort to me in the coming event as she will help my dear Kitty.

Fri 8th After we had been to Wakefield's drapery in the morning, we all set to work vigorously. We shut ourselves in little back room so as not to cause suspicion by so much work about, and Alice helped Kate and me cut out four chemises.

Sat 9th I sent for Miss Truman and gave her order for five dresses. She didn't seem surprised I was to be married. Mr Cornwall called and we told him, he wished me much happiness and promised not to tell. It is decided for them to go to Lechlade, poor dear man, he doesn't like it. I made him promise to make our house his home when he comes here. Had letter from Capt, having received my affirmative, and he is greatly rejoiced. He says he will come on Wednesday and bring Minnie to school, this was followed by another letter in the afternoon, very nice and soothing, to confirm it. I wrote to say we have arranged to go to London on Monday and perhaps he'll come to town too. Charles, Kate and I went into study to get our papers and looked out the ones to take with us. Charles wrote to Wassell and King to be trustees, and Charles will be one, then he wrote to Mullens asking him to meet him at 9½ Monday morning. Wassell had already written to Charles and begged him 'to make the dear child comfortable as you can.' I wrote to him, he doesn't quite like the engagement and wants me to make purchase in Bath. After Emma had gone to bed and we knew she couldn't guess what is happening, dear Kitty helped me mark all the Capt's shirts and collars that he left here.

Mon 11th Rose early after having spent night at our friends the Keyworths. Mrs K quite startled when I told her of my forthcoming marriage and even more so when she learnt it was Capt and not John, for she likes him much. She asked me if I had told him of it, and I said No. I was sadly depressed by the thought of having to tell it to him. Mr Mullens gave me his best wishes, and said shares must be sold and reinvested to make marriage settlement on me, he didn't advise bank shares. At station noticed that the Cooks and Burges and Bess Coles all went first class, while we went second, by excursion rates, but got on nicely. Left Cirencester at 10 and reached Paddington about 4.

Tues 12th   Sarah and I had to sleep in attic, Randall's quite full, but the Coopers left today for India and another lady, quite single, sailed for India and on to China. Mrs Davis and Gertrude came this morning. Mr Wassell and Sarah went to St Paul's to look at the windows. Mrs Davis fell in road crossing on Ludgate Hill and I ran in front of cab to pick up her parasol. A kind workman looked out for opportunity for me to cross again to join her at the chemist's shop. I was quite shaken to see how bruised her face was and Gertrude quite hysterical, so had to give her a shake. Mr Wassell said he wouldn't leave us again if that is what we got up to, so came with us to Oxford Street. He got quite irritable so I helped him pay the 6/- fare. There I purchased muslin dress, Honiton sleeves and collar for the wedding, then dined nearly opposite. Afterwards bought light boots and white dress shoes, we then parted with Mrs Davis and Gertrude, and we walked back. Kidd was waiting to see me. Charles had told him of my intended marriage this morning and he came to say that he'll bet 10,000 to 10 that it never takes place. He says I shan't have Capt, for he (Kidd) will have me himself!

Thurs 14th   Cross with Mr Wassell yesterday as he would have me go to exhibition and I had so many letters to deal with, otherwise I would have enjoyed it. Rose at 6 this morning, rained hard till 9, then set off for Littles and ordered two white grenadines and other things. Kidd still harping on telling Charles he is set on having me himself. Very hot in train on way home and it was very full. Capt met us at station and Charles had to go to settle at Mullens, Jonathan asked me about settlement and I said I had to leave all that to my brother. Emma gave us most warm welcome home.

Fri 15th   Mrs Keyworth was most anxious that Mr Davis should know as soon as possible about my marriage, but he was at Northleach when she sent Alice. Kate and I went to Miss Truman about my dress, she made me cross saying the grenadine must be matched and said many other things which annoyed me and I spoke my mind to her. I reminded her of making me get more for the last dresses and never used it, she soon came to her senses and was civil. I had a violent headache in the evening and was obliged to lie down. Capt bathed my head so gently with vinegar and carried me up to bed and came to see me when I was in bed. Dear fellow, he was so gentle and delicate. I wrote hasty note to Mr East to tell him of anticipated marriage with Capt, 'twas fixed for him to take Minnie to school tomorrow. She had been so wild and tiresome, but tonight was quite subdued. She said, 'Are you laughing, Papa?' He said, 'No, dear, I cannot laugh when I am so grieved at my Minnie's bad behaviour.' She told Kate when she was putting her to bed that she wished she was her real Aunt, and said to her that she wished her Papa would marry again as she should then have a home, and would Kate marry her Papa if he asked her.

Sat 16th   Capt started at 6½ for Northleach then hired horse to go on to Blockley with Minnie. Sarah Cornwall came and spoke sharply to Kate about her father's not being able to keep horse at Lechlade, so much so that dear Kate shed tears, and Susan was so sorry, they soon made it up. Poor Susan is much worried. I took her round garden and told her my news, it so surprised her that she wept. Then the Fluxes arrived for tea, they have taken house at Chesterton Terrace for a month. Kate and I ran over to the Frises to acquaint them with my movements and invited them to breakfast, she is expecting addition to family soon so fears it will prevent her coming, though much pleased with the invitation. Poor Emma wept when she came to our room and hinted at so much going on that I told her of my engagement. She was quite overcome and declared she loved Capt better than Mr Davis – though I seem to recall it was the other way round not so long ago. Went with Charles to tell the news to Uncle and Aunt B.T. She polite but declined the invitation. He said nothing, except that he would have to have a day or two to think about it.

Mon 18th   Capt and Charles went to London first class by excursion train, Kate and I went with them to Cirencester but had no quiet time. Had to hurry to get the licence, I fell in Castle Street and was much soiled. Went to Bowlys and bought silk dress, drugget and stair carpet. Dined at William Flux's junior at Chesterton Terrace. Charles was cross at having to miss cricket match in park. I was shocked at Mrs Flux's temper. George said aloud at least for me to hear 'I want to p...' She rose and slapped him several times and thrust him out of the room. He threw himself down on mat and she asked William to go as he resisted the door. He went and slapped him too, it grieved me much. We then went on to Mrs Keyworth and she said John had been there and just gone out. I didn't know what to do as he came back for tea almost immediately and came to sit by me. I felt so excited and from his easy manner knew he had no knowledge of what was about to take place and it pained me. I sought counsel and strength from above. We all went into drawing room, Ed Locke was there and they played baggatelle and then we passed each other on the stairs and he made to detain me. I asked if he could come to Fairford and he said he could not, so I asked him to come into the paper room. He immediately closed the door, but I held out and asked if he had heard of any news about me. He said NO, then I told him. He was very quiet at first and then said, 'Then it really is so.' He wished me every happiness. I said our intercourse had been of a peculiar nature. Not only had the Arlington people been averse to it, but it seemed as if Providence had overruled it. He said he thought so too. He said many other nice things and that he would like to continue our friendship and would come to see Kate after I left, and me when I returned to Fairford. He gave me a kind and affectionate farewell and we parted as Mrs Keyworth announced that Mr Cook had been looking everywhere for him. She didn't say anything about where we were so they knew nothing about it. I felt relieved I had told him, but felt strong inward emotions while doing so which I found hard to conceal. He also felt it much. Charles had ordered a new suit to be made at Lake's.

Tues 19th   Alice went to Miss Trumans this morning. She spoke so slightingly of the dresses, said they were coarse. We felt so vexed especially as she fitted me nearly a week ago and has not put a stitch to any one of them yet, so after dinner I went there and asked her how it was, told her I thought she was not quite pleased about something and begged her to say if I was right. Of course, she denied anything and said she was never taken to about her manner before. I said we had all noticed it every time I've seen her and thought it was perhaps because she hadn't the ordering of the dresses. She then said she wished we had let her find them as they had put such an enormous profit on them. She also as good as told me that Miss Lane's were better and prettier than mine. We had a long set to, but parted well enough at last and she promised to come up tomorrow and try pattern on. I then went to tea at the Cornwalls.

Fri 22nd   Miss Truman has been greatly benefited by my lecture to her and has done everything she was wished to and was most pleasant. Every day brings loving epistles from Capt and Kittie speaks of his kind attentions to her, she is much better and really enjoying herself. Folks keep thinking it is dear Kittie that the Capt is to marry as they still talk of my marrying dear J. He told Ellen when she went to Arlington that he should like to get into a corner to see the marriage

143

where no eye should see him. It makes my heart heavy to think of his sadness and he is so much on my mind that though I wouldn't have things otherwise now, I can't help feeling depressed. Everyone is sending congratulations and good wishes, but so many think it is for dear J, it is all quite confusing.

Sun 24th   Have had busy few days, busy at accounts and writing letters. Ran to see J Iles, she's in a precarious state. Had most loving letter from dear Capt that it makes me want to see him again, but I am astonished at myself as I do not feel at all excited over it. Told old Parr the other day and he said he should like to make the bouquet for me. He likes the Capt very much, says he has a good face. Went over the way to chapel it being the commemoration of the great St Bartholomew's Day 1662.

Mon 25th   Had hasty note from dear J to say he would walk over this morning and to put green door open. I watched in summer house for him and just giving him up when in he walked and we met in gravel walk. Charles had gone to Cirencester, but I couldn't go as Uncle B.T. wouldn't spare the horse, saying he wanted to thresh the wheat and take it to market and so took Tom as well. It was most inconvenient as I had important affairs to discuss with Mullens, but was excited that dear J came. After dinner we went up to summer house and sat on settee to talk. Emily, Kate and Ellen went into front parlour. John was kind and spoke kindly of Capt, said he seems a nice man but couldn't understand how I could have done it all up so quickly and said he didn't think I would have him, even at this

The Green Door opening onto the garden

late stage. I felt the truth of our feelings and was somewhat relieved by the tea bell ringing. In the evening Miss Truman came to fit dresses on and equipped me in full wedding attire, wreath, veil and all and all were pleased with the effect and sent me in to Charles who was back and in the dining room. Dear J came in from visiting Frise and Kate told him I was dressed in my bridal gown and would he like to see me. He turned hastily and shut himself in back parlour without a candle. Poor dear fellow, my heart ached for him. We later tried to be cheerful and had a little music and singing.

Wed 27th Signed deeds at Mullens yesterday and Charles and I met the Capt. He fitted a ring and guard to my finger. Dear Kittie gave me most handsome worked chair pieces which I like extremely. Charles gave me silver anchor brooch and one for Kate too. Yesterday was his birthday. Capt and I today agreed to go to Reading Wednesday for day or two, thence to London and then Ireland.

Thurs 28th Most lovely weather come at last. Emily, Kate and I gathered verbena and sent to flower show. Had third prize for broad beans, second for peas and plums and second for mangold wurzel. People all very friendly. Introduced Capt to Susan Cornwall and S Iles as they requested it. Thought Capt cool and almost indifferent which worried me, not that I doubt his love, but it causes me to feel at a distance. I cannot make the first advance or seek him if he doesn't seek me. Mr Reynolds and his sister came to tea and walked round garden, Being the only evening disengaged, Capt and I supped at the Frises.

Fri 29th Susan Cornwall came to see my trousseau. She said she was pleased with the Capt. At 7 the members arrived and went round garden then into dining room for tea, twenty of them came. I hear they all wondered what was up and fancied Capt had something to do with it, then Charles gave them a hint of it and very many hearty and sincere good wishes were expressed for us both. Many shed tears and Cath Mitchell went quite hysterical in the kitchen. It was 9 o'clock before they left. Hannah Vincent, old mischief maker, I hear induced Betty Miller not to come, and she said to Mrs Page and Mary 'You're not wanted, so you needn't go.' Poor Richard Page was quite disturbed about it. I felt myself happy in giving so much pleasure by giving the tea to Christ's poor but dear ones.

Sat 30th Mrs Wassell wrote to say she'd be here today, so Kate went to meet her. Dear girl, she is remarkably anxious that all should be in first rate order for me. Mrs Wassell brought a beautiful little handkerchief for me and one for Kate and a bag to put nightdress in. Alice and Ellen came too.

⚓ SEPTEMBER ⚓

Mon 1st   This has indeed been a bustling day. Charles went to Cirencester and Mrs Wassell, Cecily and Kate Howard returned with them by Collett. They brought me lovely handkerchief from their Ma with the request that I should use it on my wedding day, so I must use it and Mrs Wassell's together. They also gave me a pretty little blotting case. All so happy and kind. I was amazingly upset to find Capt's name oughtn't to have been on wedding cards and we had to write and order more, without ties. It is a great pity for those we have are so pretty, but ties are not used now. Mrs Iles from Asylum came over and walked round garden to talk to me. The Fluxes called but happily didn't stay tea. Mrs Frise came and worked a bit to help. I gave her £1 as I felt I was giving it to the Lord and not to her. She later brought me a chaste biscuit china butter dish. Capt keeps in study knowing how busy we all are. Called on Mrs Burge but not asked in as she was washing children, but she called out her good wishes. Visit to Aunt B.T. She was most gracious, though she said she thought she was not quite pleased with the Capt. My heart turned wondering her objection, then she said he shouldn't take the good away, they were not to be spared as so few of them. She asked us to stay tea, so couldn't refuse after that compliment. Mrs Savory called, she said the Capt was the right one come at last, finally called on Sue Cowley and Mrs Parr. All smiled kindly and wished us well.

Tues 2nd   Poor Harriet stung in palm of hand and it is much swollen. Mrs Wassell and Mrs Keyworth here, busy cooking. I couldn't begin packing until last night. Dear Mary Macanthy brought me handsome pebble bracelet, Mrs Keyworth an elegant device of inkstand under glass shade. Dear Alice brought a pretty basket which she lined and quilted herself, and Ellen gave me a pretty pomatum pot. I was quite overcome receiving so much. The crockery all came by Collett and all have been washing it. Old Parr busy ornamenting the dining room with evergreens, then friends set the breakfast and it looked lovely. I gave Francis a waistcoat and cravat and gloves, Richard gloves, and Emma a white cap and dress.

Wed 3rd   The all auspicious but solemn day come at last. I breakfasted in bed. Charles and Capt slept at Browns. Minnie came from Arlington by Spenser this morning looking very pretty in her book muslin dress, narrow flounces, cape of same fastened behind with two rosettes of blue, blue sash, hair nicely curled and a pretty little hat with blue and white feathers. She addressed me as Mama. The sudden title seemed rather novel and a little strange. My bridesmaids were in white grenadine with pink trimming and sashes, with pink and white hawthorn wreaths and tulle veils. They looked really lovely and charming. My own dress, a handsomely worked muslin, with clematis and orange blossom wreath and lace veil. I had a laugh at my pretty bridesmaids that out of six not one dressed me but dear Mrs Wassell. I felt very composed until, when alone, my eye caught sight of a small parcel on my dressing table addressed 'For dear Sarah, a bridal gift from her dear Katie'. I opened it with throbbing heart and it so over-came me when I saw a beautiful gold chain that I couldn't restrain my tears. Her tender love for me is so great and her kindness, that my heart yearns for her, oh, that I was more worthy of her love. When she came to my room we kissed each other but our hearts were too full for utterance and we were obliged to separate. At 10½ we all went down, the gents all gone to chapel over the way, then Charles followed with me and my bridesmaids followed. Kind friends had laid carpet down for us to walk from our door across the road to the chapel. We were all stationed in table seat and Mr Wassell and Mr Frise faced us, then the former gave address and performed the cere-mony. He didn't ask me to say I would *Obey* he said nothing about it and I enjoyed the fun of it. A funny little incident occurred which still more amused me and I couldn't refrain from smiling. As Capt was taking the ring from the little box it fell from his fingers to the ground and they had a hunt for it, I was surprised at my own calmness

The Baptist Chapel, Fairford

throughout the service. Once I felt my veil shake considerably, but all said I spoke out boldly and distinctly and gave me excellent character for going through it well. When we went to sign in vestry, the whole party came and kissed me. Then we retraced our steps and my eye caught Mrs Savory and Mrs Burge as we came out and I bowed to them as they recognised me. I saw no one else but heard the chapel was full. The photographer from Cirencester was to come to take the whole group but we were sadly disappointed and at last agreed that the six bridesmaids should be taken together and Capt and I would get ours done while away from home. Mr Mullens came to breakfast which looked first rate and all passed off exceedingly well. Richard requested to wait at table and also Emma. She was quite excited and delighted with my new name and the novelty of it made her often try to address me by it, though she forgot often as well. Mr Wassell made a speech and we did nothing but laugh, it seemed so silly. Mr Mullens left soon having several ladies waiting for him. Then the disagreeable parting came. At 3½ we left in fly and pair for Swindon, the girls all smothered me with kisses till I felt bewildered and they all followed me out to chaise. We watched them till they were out of our sight, they all looked so pretty and happy. My dear brother too did admirably and was quite cheerful to the last. I mustn't forget to say that I was requested to stick the knife into the wedding cake, passed to me for the purpose, then the six maids and Minnie gave it an extra push. However, the knife made no advance and dear Charles sawed the top then cut a large slice out, we took a piece of it to give to friends. A gentle shower fell as we drove off, but we made good journey and reached Swindon soon after 6 o'clock and were soon in first class carriage bowling on to Oxford. My dear husband was most kind and attentive to all my wants. Reaching Oxford we jumped into omnibus and stopped at hotel, but were told they couldn't take us in as they were quite full, then to a second and the third could do no better. A lady in omnibus advised us to try lodgings just opposite where she got out and we were very comfortably located. It had a pleasant sitting room and a bedroom opening from it. At 10 my spirits failed me, but I concealed it and we had reading and a prayer before we retired.

✻ ✻ ✻

The diary ends abruptly at this point. In view of the frank and intimate entries it is likely that Sarah would wish to conceal it from her newly-wed husband. The only other diary that has come to light is one for 1865, but the entries are sparse and more notelike than the earlier ones. The gap of two years may easily have been that the birth of her baby, eight months after her marriage, and her new status as wife and mother took up all of her time. In the back of the 1865 diary Sarah noted purchases and sales of shares for both 1863 and 1864 which would indicate that she did not write a diary for either of those two 'missing' years.

Having been privy to her private thoughts and revelations for so long, it is somewhat of a pity that we cannot vicariously share her experience of motherhood, for she was then thirty-eight years old, a somewhat mature age for a first child in early Victorian times. The child, born on 15 May 1863 was named after her half brother – Charles Kingsley, but she refers to him in the diary as Kingsley, no doubt to distinguish between him and Charles who was still spending a lot of time at Milton House where Sarah and Captain Milbourne settled. Kate and Mr Davis still feature in Sarah's life and there are sufficient snippets in the entries for the story to be pieced together.

1865

❧ JANUARY ❧

Sun 1st Baby very poorly, feared measles, eyes very heavy and a severe cold. Mrs Frise and Faulkes came in to see him and think him very sadly.

Mon 2nd Emma had good news from home, 'Father been to London, and is quite well'. Two hours later, Smith's coal waggon stopped at the door to say she must be ready to return with it as her father was very, very ill. She went, 'twas bitterly cold. Baby still poorly, cried for two hours evidently in pain, had never done so before. Kate very poorly, so Rhoda and I staid in front parlour all night with him.

Tues 10th Kingsley much better and has been out several days. Charles walked little way with Mr Davis when he returned this afternoon and spoke to him about a settlement on Kate, which he said he expected. Kate better and walked with Rhoda, Minnie, self and baby to Whelford. Uncle B.T. there for a while, little Kingsley put up his face to kiss him, but the old gent turned his face away. We each had a letter from Capt, and are thankful to hear his health is better, indeed good, and that he is coming home March or April, but evidently thinks of going back again. The letter was registered to me, brought by Manning. Mrs Bragg of Milbourne House, Stroud wrote today for May Walker's character.

Sat 14th Good news from Australia this morning. Charles and I sat a long time talking things over with Kate. I long and pray for her happiness and cannot reconcile to turn of events.

Mon 16th Minnie's birthday. We all gave her presents. Aunt Kate a large bouncing ball, I a white fur neck tie, a little diary from her Papa and 2/6d stamps from her Grandma. Miss Hobbs sent a carte de visite, but this has been a most trying day. Minnie gave me a great pain again and particularly as I tried hard to give her pleasure. She ended up quite penitent and I forgave her, then I was obliged to chastise our own dear boy also. Mrs Moreton called, she makes a great fuss of Kingsley, calls him the little Saxon boy. Kate quite middling.

Sat 21st Dear Tom has been gone ten months today. Poor Ann Watts taken to the asylum at Gloucester. We went in coburg to Lechlade to the Cornwalls, Mrs in bed so didn't see her. Mr Cornwall, naughty man, would give baby a wee taste of ginger wine though I said his Papa wouldn't like it. Then called on Mrs Croucher, she made loud complaints of the Rev Mr Rice and family being too proud and not doing more in Fairford. Wrote our letters to Africa this evening.

Fri 27th Very few horses out, travelling so dangerous after snow then the severest frost of the winter, worst for many years. Mr Davis staid overnight on Tuesday, he told us more of Ann Arkell. She acts most disgustingly, then says she shall go to church and leave chapel, good riddance, too, they are welcome to her. Baby amusing himself with little talk, behaved himself very well at chapel on Sunday. Saw in the paper that African mail steamer 'Armenian' is wrecked off Wesford on Arklow sands. Also reported was the loss of the West Indian Pacific steamer, with the loss of several lives, some of whom tried to save others from ill-fated 'Armenian' and four from the lightship.

FEBRUARY

Wed 1st Snow fast going now, but it has been intensely cold. Charles and Minnie went to 'high place' last Sunday and wouldn't come over the way to chapel with me. Charles wrote to ask Mr Hope the lowest price at which shares in African Company of Merchants can be had. They were quoted at ½ discount. Heard the Ethiope sailed yesterday in lieu of the 'Armenian'. Feel anxious that another vessel should have sailed to Africa and we not know it though we have kept close watch in the Star. Poor 'Armenian', it is the same vessel dear Capt brought home from Sierra Leone this time last year, and was so behind after he left for Africa in March that we did not get news of his reaching Madeira for several weeks. She had met there with some misfortune.

Mon 6th Mr Davis came to Ruth Ballinger for tea then here. He and Kate had a sore trouble and I acted as mediator. After all had gone to bed I talked to him long and hard, and begged him to commit it to prayer before he melted my heart. He did so and seemed chastened to me, but poor Kittie had much cause for complaint.

Fri 10th Had short note from my dear Tom, says nothing about returning except in one he enclosed for his sister Bessie, in that he said March. Kate and I put our personal accounts right, so nothing left to pay either now. Settled with Frise £1 for tuning piano. Had long talk with Rhoda. She says Miss Clappen has offered her £20 a year and evidently is trying to get me to pay her same, but I resisted and she is now quite humbled. George Clissold came yesterday and staid night, he and Charles settled their accounts between them up to last Christmas, George for rent, Charles for beer. In Capt's letter he said the plum pudding was delicious and the wedding cake quite a novelty. Found poor Mrs Hewer without a servant and poor Johnnie with a broken chilblain. Mr Moreton called yesterday and invited himself to tea next week. Very busy pastry making for the Dorcas meeting to be held here, then only three came.

Wed 15th Bessie Coles married today to her cousin William Yells at his home. A grief to her sister Mary Anne as he is not steady.

Sun 19th Snow deeper than before and still bitterly cold. Today brings the matter of John's supplying for the church. We pray for him. I went over the way to chapel as we couldn't get to Meysey Hampton, but Kate and Charles preferred to stay home, unhappy atmosphere in evening as my going there caused them great offence.

Mon 20th Mr Davis came as snow is starting to thaw. He says all were unanimous for him to remain pastor at Arlington, even when he is married and lives here, at least for a time. The church accepted Mr Belcher's resignation.

Wed 22nd Rapid thaw so was able to get to Quenington to see about the orphan children Kent, there being a vacancy in the orphan asylum at Bristol for two girls.

Thurs 23rd Charles, Kate, Mr Frise and I went to Cirencester to the Union and saw the four Kents. Our hearts ached for them, they were starved with the cold. Saw Parsons and spoke very plainly to him of his state as a sinner.

Sat 25th   Kate bought a dozen towels and a brown dress for us both from Wakefields. Took a lot of old clothes to give to the poor people of Meysey Hampton, then sent Francis to meet Mr Stratford. After supper we had the box of dear Grandpapa's[44] letters and manuscripts in back parlour and looked them over. We had a most pleasant evening. John came and staid night. Charles had to go to Uncle B.T.'s about selling part of land to Railway Company, it seemed an unpleasant business.

❧ MARCH ☙

Wed 1st   Charles again had to see about the selling of the land then drove Kate, Rhoda, children and me to Arlington. I called on Ann Arkell and spoke my mind plainly to her about her conduct, then we tead at John's and spent a pleasant time. Charles called on the Moreton's on our return and returned the burnt bible.

Sat 4th   Minnie very naughty at her music last night and again this morning at her reading. So much so that we went without her for a walk with the baby. Saw the hunters come across the road, a better sight than I had ever seen before. I felt truly grieved that my beloved Minnie was so naughty as to be kept at home instead of being with us to enjoy the sight of it. Sent remittance to Messrs Cornwall and Barnes for their bill: self £1 3s; Kate £1 11s 6d.

Wed 8th   I hardly know what course to take with Minnie, she is most hardened. Day after day she is so trying, then when spoken to of her fault she cries most passionately and makes most foolish appeals for pity, but I dare not give way to her. She is so stubborn about her lessons, and is trying always to get the upper hand. She acts so deceitfully and tells falsehoods. I am anxious. She does not feel the shame and sorrow the case demands, such as when she said she could not read the word 'Josiah' and appealed to God to witness that she could not read it.

Sun 12th Now I have trouble with Rhoda. Emma told me that Rhoda with several others says she believes she is converted and nothing shall keep her from being baptised and join the chapel over the way. I can't but regret it as I don't believe she is converted as only a week ago when making the beds with her she told me she was not converted and it at once set her against George Sly as he is a member and ought not therefore to think of her. I told her she was quite right. Then when she referred a few minutes to the subject before Emma, Emma said 'Ah, Mrs Milbourne, she says that because she wants Edwin Smith.' I told her the same thing would apply.

Wed 15th Mr Davis has been here for the last few days and wants Kate to fix the time, she named the last week in May. Emma told me in confidence that Rhoda is going to see Mr Frise about being baptised and says that nothing shall hinder her from joining the chapel. It worries me as I do not think Rhoda is a changed character. I wonder she does not name it to me as she knows we are most interested in her. I know Charles will not like it and Kate and I shall have the credit of it.

Mon 20th Minnie still tries me sadly and does not seem to care one jot for having told the lie beyond the inconvenience of the punishment I am obliged to mete out. Had to reprove Rhoda for being rude and she is very disagreeable. Much saddened to see Charles's account overdrawn. Lent him £1 5s to go to Cirencester by Collett, paid Mr Smith £10 for preaching and settled Brown for gas £1 5s.

Mon 27th Annoyed with Uncle B.T. he treated our application for the horse on Wednesday with contempt. He has it today himself and Charles has gone with him to Cirencester to settle financial affairs. When I showed Charles the account he became quite ill and I had to revive him with brandy. Aunt B.T. very poorly and is quite brown. Mr Cornwall has been sent for. Emma says Rhoda very angry that Mr Frise has not taken any notice of her so she thinks she shall let the matter of baptism drop. I in turn was angry to learn that Frise had told Rhoda that Mr and Mrs Davis would be living here after they marry as I had not named it to them. She said Mrs Frise does not like John coming here. Little Anna very ill with congestion of the lungs.

❧ APRIL ☙

Tues 4th Charles walked to Hatherop and Quenington to get signatures from the relatives of the orphan children Kent. Finding out from the farm men that the horse wasn't very busy, we sent for it but Uncle B.T. crossly and firmly refused it and said we should never ask the men about it. He came to Francis this morning and went to take the wheelbarrow out of his hands while he was wheeling manure to the hot bed and said he should not have had it, then he told Joe he had no master. It is all so distressing. Then Mrs Iles called and I told her Kate was to be married. She had not heard of it and wanted to know ins and outs from Kate later when they went collecting for the Dorcas Society.

Mon 10th Kate and I went to Cirencester, but could find no dress suitable for her. We bought a silver cruet stand at Tanners 78/-. Poor Mrs Keyworth very sadly. I fear she is not long for this world, but I don't think she is alive to the fact of her real state. No letter from Africa, though the winds have been favourable. Mrs Price came to work.

Sat 15th News in the Morning Star that Richmond is taken by the Federals and I trust now the war will soon cease. I begin to feel very anxious about African mail not arriving. Kate and I went to see Mrs Moreton about their son. She told us there is another little White coming. John came this morning and wasn't in first rate humour. He was cross with me about a trifle, but misunderstood me and all old feelings flowed back and put me in a fix, but commonsense prevailed and it was all right at last, but a thoroughly bad hour. Caldicott came by appointment and we agreed he should come to begin the back parlour the week after next.

Thurs 20th Charles wrote to Tobin by this morning's mail to make enquiries about the missing mail and we heard from dear Tom this afternoon by coincidence. All is well. Kate and I cleared museum then went to see Mr Barnes's house, went for walk with Rhoda, Minnie and little Kingsley before the Howards came at 7.

Tues 25th Miss Wakefield married here this morning. Mr Cornwall called and seemed most fatherly towards me. Kate and Charles went to Faringdon and Rhoda and I set to work and took down our bed furniture and Charles sent the last to wash. Rhoda and Emma washed ours with machine and several articles besides and dried all, then I began rockery in garden.

Wed 26th   Very busy day. Painters, plasterers, carpenters. Had two bed furniture down, had one and window set washed at home and turned it. Minnie helped. Out of sending for four to come ironing, only Mrs Brown could oblige. Just as I was sitting down to dinner off bacon, Mr Ferris came and dined off it too, with broccoli and cold apple pie then tead at Frises. Sent Minnie to get a £20 cheque cashed at Wakefields and she brought back only £5, so sent her back and 'twas soon put right.

Fri 28th   This morning, looking in yesterday's paper, to my dismay saw 'The assassination of Lincoln', for some time could not regain my composure, saw also Constance Kent has confessed to murdering her half brother Saville Kent and given herself up to justice. While we were busy working hard and fast, dear Kitty and John returned from London. They were surprised beyond belief at what was accomplished in their absence.

Sun 30th   Mr Stratford's tract of Gloucestershire Men, and especially of John Thomas, our revered grandfather, came this morning. I like it much. I feel dismayed to think how fast the wedding draws nigh and how much there is to do.

❧ MAY ❧

Mon 1st   Kate and I went to Wakefields and chose dresses for Emma and Rhoda, at least they both chose grenadine at 8d a yard. After early lunch we went to Cirencester to take Kate's wedding dress to Miss Hooper. Bought set of tea trays at Alexanders for 30/-. At Maces we bought a dozen tumblers 8/6d; a dozen wine glasses 8/6d and a set of tea things for £2.

Thurs 4th   Kate and I began clearing out lower room and a dirty job it was. Charles returned from London by coach. Emily wanted to come tonight but had to put her off as the painters have not finished.

Mon 8th   Charles and Kate to see Mullens in Cirencester in reference to her marriage settlement. John came over and helped me brush back bedroom furniture and alter locks, he was very kind and useful. Mrs Rice with work all about in front parlour doing my white dress up for

24th and all the boxes and packages in dining room, 'twas a regular bedlam with the painters finishing back parlour. Just when John was helping me with the children to do a little garden, lo, the two Miss Iles's called, closely followed by Mr Cornwall. Heavy thunderstorm during night so had little sleep and tired out.

Sun 14th Received a telegram this morning from my precious husband to say he had reached Liverpool safely and would come on at once. So, after early dinner, went to Cirencester to meet him, and took Emma to see her father. Mr Keyworth and Orlando went to Tetbury Road station to meet dear Capt. I was overjoyed to have him home once more safe and sound. He brought a monkey for Charles from Sierra Leone, a parrot for Mrs Keyworth and Minnie and a lot of pineapples.

Wed 24th (Queen Victoria's birthday). Kate's wedding day. My spirits very sadly. Harriet came to help as she did at mine, but was not well. Kate went through it well. I felt very hysterical just as we started but recovered soon.

There are no entries for the next couple of weeks and the diary starts again when they are obviously in Paris. It is strange that Sarah has not noted why they went or when.

᚛JUNE᚜

Sun 18th Capt, Charles, Kate, John and self went to Madeleine Church and were pained and sickened at the idolatory, felt ashamed of ourselves for being there. The gents went in afternoon to Baptist church and communed with them. Before the service was over a grand procession commenced. About 100 little girls all dressed in white, with white caps and a garland of flowers on their heads, and a bouquet in their hands, came from the left side of the altar, closely followed by some 100 older girls all in white book muslin, with white caps and veils partly covering the face. The first two carried a handsome white silk banner, and every dozen or so after carried one also. They were followed by as many little boys, with broad bands of white ribbon on one arm and all with bouquets, as also the procession of men who followed them, and last of all the host. It took a long time as they frequently stopped in the church and then the same ceremony proceeded round the outside, preceded by a brass band. We felt saddened and disgusted by the scene, although pretty and imposing in itself. The gents were pleased with the communion service in the Baptists little room and the members, though all French, gave them a hearty welcome. The males saluted each other on both cheeks, and the females did the same.

Mon 19th Mr Lepoids breakfasted with us at our hotel, he afterwards took us to see the Tomb of Napoleon.

Tues 20th We all went to the Louvre, the paintings were splendid, but so many on one subject, crucifixion. Tom had to go out on business, I felt very poorly and had to lie down.

Sun 25th In evening went to Kingsgate Street. Kate and John went to see Dr Cummings and Capt and I called on Mr Berry at Holborn. He left Africa since Tom and says a fearful epidemic is raging there and named a great many who were known to Capt who are dead since he returned. I felt very sick and giddy on our return and left Charles with Capt.

Tues 27th Capt had to have his ears syringed, I have been so poorly and sick that I long to get home.

The Church of St Thomas of Canterbury, Horcott

⚓ JULY ⚓

Tues 4th Dear Capt left this morning by Collett for Liverpool.

Wed 19th Capt returned unexpectedly. We thought he might come back by Collett. The Cooks and Mrs Locke came to dine and joked me about sea sickness as I am still suffering badly from sickness. Charles left this morning for London and Maidstone to give his vote. We feel anxious about him as at Cheltenham and at Chippenham blood has been shed. I had to write to Mrs Gopsill Brown, Belle Vue House, Gloucester as she wanted Rhoda's character. I told her she was engaged here to Michaelmas. Tom, Minnie and I took baby across the Green and into park. Took baby's shoes and socks off in the Green and put his feet in the water of the little stream, which he much enjoyed.

⚓ AUGUST ⚓

Thurs 3rd Dear Capt and I took Minnie to school this morning. Drove to Arlington and hired Spencer's horse and cart as his horse would not go in shafts of coburg. We had a few storms and thunder while we called on friends. Reached Chipping Norton soon after 8, Miss Beal gave us warm welcome. I had begged Minnie to pray that she should love the truth.

Fri 4th We left for Bradford at 11. I went first and bought Minnie a silk jacket. She seemed grieved because she was to be advanced to another class, as she would have more work to do. I asked Miss Beal to be strict with her. At Didcot had to wait three hours, then at Bath had tea at Mr Wassell's old lodgings and got to Bradford soon after 7.

Sun 6th Dear Capt spoke to the people this morning and gave a lecture in the evening about Africa, and a few words to schoolchildren in afternoon.

Fri 11th Spent much time visiting old friends. Bought a leg bath for 7/-. Heard from Kate and she seemed better, says they have bought a pony for £8. I still feel distressed about poor dear Kate. Tom went to Southampton yesterday and we went to sale at Sedgehill. A shade has been cast over us as dear Tom has received telegram calling him to Liverpool. Then one came for him to see steamer sold in London, followed by yet another to say he was not needed in London.

Sat 12th   Dear Tom left early this morning, Mr King driving him to station. Annie went too as they had to go on to Shaftesbury on business.

Mon 14th   This has been a trying day. As we retired last night, Mr King came to our door and said softly that the steps were placed up to the girls' window. It was blowing high. He sat down in the kitchen waiting the result. Emma's sweetheart was suspected as they had been told that he had been seen coming from here early Monday morning in best clothes and steps were often at her window. Many schemes were proposed. Mine was to go with Annie up to her room and catch them as she might make mischief if Mr King went. But Mr King thought it best if he would drop something and make a noise to startle them out of bed. He would then go to the outhouse and would see him come out of her window and pass him close by without being seen. Annie and I half dressed. Then, most strangely, while hesitating and asked direction of God, a ginger beer bottle cork burst. They roused, but soon hushed to sleep again. We then had another consultation in Mrs King's room, we said we would go down and pretend to light a fire and make noise with kettle. I went stumping upstairs with candle and asked Emma if she heard noise as Miss Down and I were sleeping together and had been startled by noise so had to look round. At this, out he bundled at the window and Mr King saw him and he tried to get out of door where Mr King had run to. It was long before we could settle to retire again. In the morning Mr and Mrs King had her in, then later I had her in my room and talked to her very seriously. I made her pray for forgiveness. She is frightened, but I do not feel truly penitent.

Thurs 24th   Returned home yesterday after much visiting in Weymouth and Berwick. Bought baby dress for 12/-, it is a holland pinafore and jacket. Flower Show in Park. John is very quiet and disagreeable and got quite angry when I tried to get him out in the evening. He seems very aloof. Dear Kate met Charles and me at Cirencester and went with me to engage Nurse Chaplam for February. She was at Viners. A lovely day today after such wet yesterday.

Fri 25th   Have had no rest or sleep. Kate and I up till 3 o'clock trying to put matters straight, but John was very formidable and tried to make his exit, but Kate restrained him. The noise on the stairs frightened Charles, but we kept counsel.

⚓SEPTEMBER⚓

Sun 3rd Three years today since dear Captain and I were married. We rose earlier than usual and engaged in prayer for our hearts are filled with deep gratitude for all the mercies we have enjoyed over those three years. The severe dangers by sea and land in which my beloved husband has been preserved to return to us again is cause for such thankfulness and encourages us to be hopeful for the future. This has been a happy day for us both.

Sat 9th My dear husband went to Liverpool today. The Mate's case as also the Capt's to be tried on Monday. The telegram came for him to go Wednesday as the Mate of Sobraom was to be tried then, but the message did not catch up with Tom until we were at Woodhouse and Keyworth sent his boy up with it. Tom telegraphed that it was impossible to get there in time. We had such a lovely day at Woodhouse, little Kingsley so enjoyed it, though Uncle B.T. was so contrary. The following day we went in intense heat to Arlington tea meeting, Kate and I quite knocked up. Dear Kate is to go with John on Monday to his mother's at Lavington.

High Street, Fairford

Tues 26th   Dear Kate and John returned home, having gone on to Bradford, poor girl, she is so unwell and has been since they were away, he in very quiet mood and I feel uneasy about it. Tom went to Baxter's sale on Saturday and spent £10 2s. 6d. Charles went with him in Miller's trap to fetch the things home after tea. Had nice penitential letter from Minnie for not writing to me since she left home and apology from Miss Beal. But then Kittie told me she had written a scolding letter to Minnie for her thoughtlessness, it rather spoiled it as I thought it was Minnie's own doing, but dear Kittie meant well as always. Minnie grieves me extremely. Wrote to William and John jointly, Capt and Charles also wrote to them.

OCTOBER

Wed 4th   Matters do not improve. Some folks went off without saying a word to poor Kate. Seemed to go off to Arlington in good enough spirits, but returned in bad mood and hardly spoke to anyone, and not a word to some.

Thurs 5th   Capt postponed his visit as unhappy circumstances here. Kate dressed at 11 and went into museum with J. While there she fainted. We got her into back bedroom, she looked so ill. Emma staid all day by her side. I later asked J how Kate was and was answered by silence and then he rose and left the table and went upstairs, saw no more of him until a creeping down the stairs in listening attitude alerted me to him. Charles went up to the little room with him and took him to task quite firmly, then dear Tom was obliged to speak to him in the study about his conduct. He spoke plainly and firmly to him and we look for a change in attitude.

Sat 7th   Tom left today for Liverpool. Sent hamper of pears, apples, grapes, walnuts, flowers and a piece of bacon to Lilly – we sent it by train. Emma left by Collett and Mary Fowler came. So many have said that they are sure she will never suit us that it seems quite vexatious.

Sat 14th   Mary was so slow at first, all meals behind and cold dinners but her pots are so clean that it seems a good token. She is coming with Kate, Charles and I and little Kingsley to Meysey Hampton chapel tomorrow. John still at Arlington so things are on even keel at the moment.

Thurs 19th   John back from Arlington. It was so wet I could not go to meet dear Tom from coach so John went instead. Mrs Wall busy squeezing grapes for wine. So delighted to have dear Capt home again, but my heart is heavy at our having to part again so soon.

Mon 23rd   Went to Cirencester with my beloved husband, drove direct to the station and had not one moment to spare before the doors were shut. I sent for nurse and engaged her for dear Kate for April, latter end.

❧NOVEMBER❧

Thurs 2nd   Dear Ma's birthday. I had to call on Mrs Wright yesterday to explain my sending for P Pyman, as she had disappointed me. She is a *strapper*. Felt low at parting with dear Kate as I left for London, bore journey better than I expected. Mrs Ebenezer Viney dined and I had long chat with her about my state, find that she suffers much as I do. Feel quite poorly again.

Mon 27th   Reached home safely on the 18th. John came to say good-bye to me yesterday while I was in bed. I didn't want him to, but it softened my heart to him, but then he was very cross with dear Kate after that. He didn't return home until supper time today and still moody.

Thurs 30th   Mrs Burge and Mrs Savory came to tea, they both say I shan't go my full time. Sam and Mr Hewer came after to sup. Kate and I have worked hard all day and Mary has done little, every place is filthy. John not home again till 7.

❧DECEMBER❧

Sat 2nd   Much dread Kate's going off to Arlington again for few days. They called on Mr Cornwall to welcome him back to Fairford, I was not well enough to go out.

Mon 4th   Mary very saucy. She did for me at last by saying that Mrs Davis offered her pig's food. It happened to be first rate potatoes which were being boiled for the pig and Kate took some and ate with relish and offered some to Mary when she came into kitchen. She said she prided herself on being better brought up than Emma or Ann Laight and had a much better home, so no wonder they didn't complain. At last, after a severe taking to she burst into tears and asked forgiveness. I think she is now very ashamed.

Sat 9th Dear Kittie back, but her face covered in rash for three days, I sent for Barnes, fearful it might be measles. Heard from Tom, safely arrived in Sierra Leone, has had bad choleraic attack, but assures me he is better now.

Fri 15th We were determined to get John to go to Mary's mother and ask her to come up this afternoon, which she did. We told her of Mary's sauce, she was rude to poor Kate the other day and said she gave her sour beer. Mrs Fowler spoke very nicely to us and went into kitchen to talk to her daughter, she also saw filthy state of the dining room.

Sun 17th Ventured to Meysey Hampton, but Kingsley so naughty and cried so much being put in the coburg that it frightened the horse. I had to chastise him on our return.

Sat 23rd Dear William's birthday. Charles heard from him this morning and he sent his likeness. Neither of us knew him, strangely altered and so old looking. He says Jonathan has been laid up for four months with rheumatic attack and has not yet joined William in consequence. Kingsley returned from ride in perambulator crying and very poorly. Minnie returned after tea, she is much grown, I wrote to dear Tom.

Christmas Day: a very quiet day. Feeling a little better walked in the garden a while, and John had the dogs out.

Wed 27th Mrs Hewer returned from Meysey Hampton with Kate and Minnie and little Kingsley. She set to and helped do back bedroom for Mrs Stephens and Ann Eliza who came by supper time. The house is so filthy in every corner that everyone is uncomfortable Mary away home for a few days and we have to clean up her mess. Mrs Frise came while we were at tea, although Kate had asked her to stay, silly little woman was so ceremonious that she wouldn't when we said Mrs Stephens was coming. John returned from Arlington tonight, wet through.

Editor's Postscript

No other diary has come to light. It is understandable that in view of the events immediately following this last one, Sarah did not record any more of her daily life.

Sarah's second child, John Seymour Milbourne was born 5 February 1866. She refers to her engaging a nurse, her 'state' and 'not going her full time'.

Kate died shortly after, on 13 May 1866. It can only be conjectured that it was through childbirth as Sarah mentions engaging a nurse for 'Kate for April, latter end'.

Sarah is remarkably guarded in her entries relating to Kate's marriage to her 'dear J', the Rev John Davis. The relationship of the two couples must have been strained at times, and Sarah infers this in her diary. From her remarks it would not seem a very happy partnership between John and Kate, which is no more than one would expect given Sarah's intense feelings for him, and his for her. Kate is buried in Fairford Baptist Chapel graveyard, as are her parents. No doubt John Davis moved away on the death of his young wife; his living at Milton House, the home of his former lover while her husband was away at sea would have been untenable.

Captain Thomas Milbourne died in November 1899, aged eighty, and is buried in the now redundant graveyard of Meysey Hampton Chapel. The chapel is now a private house. He continued the work that Sarah's father had started at Meysey Hampton and his name features in much of Fairford's commercial and educational interests: the railway, markets and school in particular. His decision to decline the post of Consul in Sierra Leone, which he was offered on Captain Burton's retirement (with whom he had shared quarters for some considerable time) can be traced back to the time of Kate's death, and that could have been the deciding factor. Sarah also probably had a hand in the decision as she then had two children of her own, and Minnie, to look after.

From registers, records and his obituary, Captain Thomas

Milbourne emerges as an interesting and able man. The son of John Milbourne, a brewer, baker and landowner of considerable family estates in Northumberland and Cumberland, including Armathwaite Castle, Thomas was born in Newcastle-upon-Tyne in 1819. By birth he was a Freeman of Newcastle-upon-Tyne and Carlisle. There was a similarity between him and Sarah's adventurous grandfather, John Thomas, in that they both ran away to sea. Thomas Milbourne obtained his Master's certificate before he became of age (20 years), but, unlike John Thomas, 'attained a great earnestness of religion' very early in his career. He offered his services to the Baptist Missionary Society who were about to send out the first missionary ship 'known to modern religious enterprise', and was appointed Master of *The Dove*, his command at that time being purely honorary. He 'safely brought the living freight of missionaries and their wives' to the West Coast of Africa, after an exciting chase by a pirate ship, *The Raven*.

He was later described as not only an explorer of the West African coast but one of the pioneers in opening up the interior, and was at Coomassi (now Ghana Gold Coast) half a generation before Sir Garnet Wolsey's famous military expedition. Among his few papers is a letter from two of the Kings of the Brass Country addressed to King Pepple of Bonny proposing to refer the settlement of 'the unhappy difference which exists between us to Thomas Milbourne, Esq, agent for the African merchants'. There is also a letter signed by King Pepple asking Captain Milbourne to see him so that 'we may settle about your going to the Bishop of London to ask him to send a missionary out here and to Palmerston about our old man-of-war for a hulk etc'.

Such was the esteem in which Captain Milbourne was held by Governor Blackwell of Sierra Leone that when, on the eve of sailing of one of the West Africa Company's steamers bearing important government despatches, the Captain went out of his mind, the Governors requested Captain Milbourne to take command. This is the 'large ship lying anchor without Master' referred to in his letter which Sarah mentions in her entry of 10 April 1861.

The voyage was not without its difficulties and dramas: a mutiny of the ship's officers termed 'a serious incident', was quelled by Captain Milbourne owing to 'him being a man of such great tact and firmness as well as of excellent justice and good nature', and he brought the ship to port with such dispatch that Lord Palmerston sent for him to thank him personally. Sarah writes of 'the Capt and Mate's case being tried' in September 1865. His declining the offer of the post as British Consul was made 'with great reluctance' and it was at this time he gave up his seafaring career and devoted himself to the simple country life in Fairford, supervising the small Baptist Chapel at Meysey Hampton, which Sarah's father had built, in close association with Charles Kingsley. He was a 'total abstainer from his earliest years'.

His obituary records him as 'a man pure and peaceable, gentle and gracious. He won to an exceptional degree the esteem of those from whom he differed, though he always firmly upheld his religious and political principles which were Liberal and loyal in the best and widest sense'.

Minnie married J W Williams, and their address was given as Leeds in 1899. Sarah died in 1905, also aged eighty. She is buried at Meysey Hampton Chapel graveyard. All her property was left equally between her two sons, except for £20 to her friend Ellen Keyworth.

Milton House, the Thomas's family home and scene of this story, was sold in 1905. It was later demolished and Fayre Court, a Cotswold small manor house, was built in the north-east corner of the sizeable garden. There are vestiges of Sarah's past still to be seen: a chestnut tree is one she would have known, the shady walks, the high garden walls, the shrubs and trees and the old coach house and stable block – and the green door, where she and 'dear J' lingered so often, and dreamed a future which was never to be. They sleep now with their secrets.

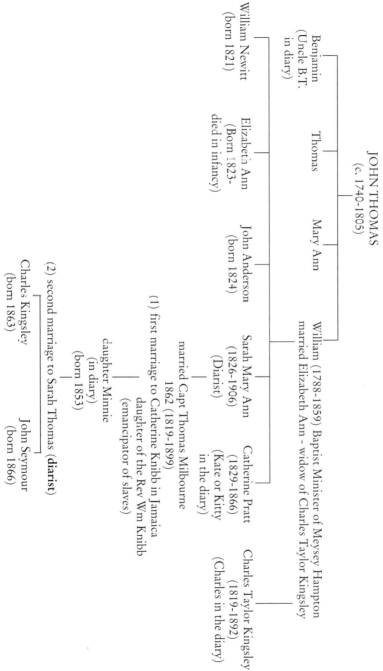

PATERNAL FAMILY TREE of SARAH THOMAS (Diarist)

JOHN THOMAS
(c. 1740-1805)

Benjamin
(Uncle B.T.
in diary)

Thomas

Mary Ann

William (1788-1859) Baptist Minister of Meysey Hampton
married Elizabeth Ann - widow of Charles Taylor Kingsley

William Newitt
(born 1821)

Elizabeth Ann
(Born 1823-
died in infancy)

John Anderson
(born 1824)

Sarah Mary Ann
(1826-1906)
(Diarist)

Catherine Pratt
(1829-1866)
(Kate or Kitty
in the diary)

Charles Taylor Kingsley
(1819-1892)
(Charles in the diary)

married Capt Thomas Milbourne
1862 (1819-1899)

(1) first marriage to Catherine Knibb in Jamaica
daughter of the Rev Wm Knibb
(emancipator of slaves)

daughter Minnie
(in diary)
(born 1853)

(2) second marriage to Sarah Thomas (**diarist**)

Charles Kingsley
(born 1863)

John Seymour
(born 1866)

171

MATERNAL FAMILY TREE of **SARAH THOMAS** (Diarist)

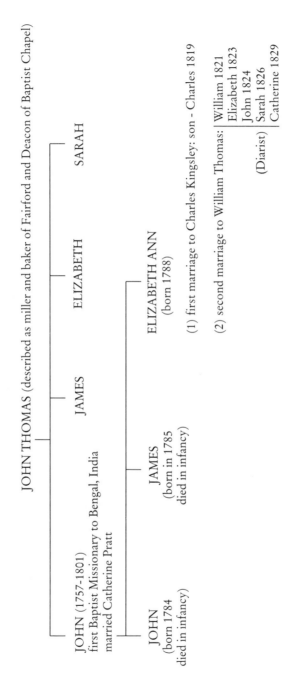

JOHN THOMAS (described as miller and baker of Fairford and Deacon of Baptist Chapel)

JOHN (1757-1801)
first Baptist Missionary to Bengal, India
married Catherine Pratt

JAMES

ELIZABETH

SARAH

JOHN
(born 1784
died in infancy)

JAMES
(born in 1785
died in infancy)

ELIZABETH ANN
(born 1788)

(1) first marriage to Charles Kingsley: son - Charles 1819

(2) second marriage to William Thomas:

William 1821
Elizabeth 1823
John 1824
Sarah 1826 (Diarist)
Catherine 1829

Notes

1 Richard Page was servant to the Thomas household. He appears also in the 1851 census, then aged sixteen years, he was born at Down Ampney.

2 The 'chapel over the road' still stands and some of the Thomas family tombs are prominent in the small burial ground which fronts the chapel. Built as a Baptist Meeting House in 1723, it was rebuilt as a chapel in 1853. When the Baptist congregation finally died out in Fairford, the Congregationalists and Baptists united and finally all non-conformists in the town amalgamated and formed the Fairford United Church, still using the old chapel in Milton Street.

3 Charles Cornwall was described as surgeon and apothecary in the census. He would have been aged about sixty-eight at the time of Sarah's writing. His second son, James, also followed in his father's profession, and is mentioned in the diary.

4 The Rev. Francis Rice, vicar of St Mary's Church, later became Lord Dynevor. The family tombs are in the churchyard and a small terrace of cottages at the west end of the town is named after him. Despite the reference in one entry to the Rices not doing much for Fairford, there is evidence in various reports that on succeeding to the baronetcy, Lord Dynevor sent 'beef and parcels of clothing to the poor of Fairford'. These, no doubt, found their way to the Anglican members and further highlights the division between the Established Church and the Non-Conformists – Sarah comments on this in her entry of 26 January 1860: 'all of them from the poor despised dissenters'.

5 Mr Smith was the preacher at Meysey Hampton Baptist Chapel, a village about three miles from Fairford. The expenses in running the chapel were borne by the Thomas family.

6 The Rev. John Frise was minister at the Baptist Chapel, Fairford. It is interesting how slightingly Sarah writes about him and his family, giving an insight of his personal life and weaknesses apparently not evident to his faithful followers. A William Hayward of Kempsford wrote a short account of the conversion of the village blacksmith which was 'so marvellous a change' that he had the village (and the vicar) 'all of a wonder at it', based on his father's recollections of the 'miracle'. This would have been contemporaneous with Sarah's diary, so it is amusing how differently they viewed Mr Frise. Sarah speaks disparagingly of his heavy smoking, his

often dubious commitment to his duties even going so far as to say he would be a better piano tuner than minister, whilst the impressed Mr Hayward of Kempsford wrote of him 'some of us were carried in arms to the (blacksmith's) shop. The place being full and I remember some of the features: the rugged seat, the iron pulpit where stood the dear saintly John Frise; a wonderful preacher as I learnt afterwards.'

7   The lunatic asylum was a private asylum, founded by Alexander Iles in 1822, when he was granted a licence 'to keep not more than ten lunatics in his own house'. It later became known as The Retreat. Patients came from all over the country and paupers were admitted to relieve the drain on the poor rate, many were employed on the Iles's farm and neighbouring gardens. The Retreat closed in 1944 and after housing a private riding stables for five years, re-opened as Coln House School for pupils with special educational needs in 1949.

8   Crofts Chapel was the Congregational Chapel. The Congregational 'Cause at the Croft' dated from the historic 1662 (mentioned as a prominent date by Sarah). The building, now demolished, was rebuilt in the Gothic style in 1862, replacing an earlier one of 1744, itself an extension of the original Meeting House. After the Congregationalists amalgamated with the Baptists, the chapel served the community in various guises: Scouts, youth clubs, drama groups and school dinners took their respective turns until it was demolished in 1965.

9   Uncle Ben Thomas, often referred to as Uncle B.T., was the older brother of Sarah's father. Benjamin Thomas married Sarah Freeman – their anniversary is recorded by Sarah. There appears to have been a long running arrangement over land and heridatments between Sarah's father and his brother Benjamin. He owned property at Burdocks, a small farming estate to the south west of the town, and some in Horcott, a hamlet of Fairford (but formerly of Kempsford parish). Benjamin was in debt to William (Sarah's father) in 1843 and a very long deed of arrangements relates to settlement of lands in Fairford.

10 The Pest House was a kind of isolation hospital for paupers – but little more than a couple of cottages at Burdocks. It was administered by the Overseers of the Poor who bought a barn for the purpose from charity funds in 1757 for £70. A second tenement was added in 1765. From the entry relating to 'Charles settling for the Pest House', it would seem that it was at this date (1860) that the building converted to cottages and into private ownership.

11 John Savory was a machine maker at Milton End. The agricultural implements suffered badly in the 'swing riots' and many of the offenders served long prison sentences, others were deported, for smashing the machinery which they saw as a threat to their livelihood in this then largely agricultural area.

12 A private girls school was run in what is now Park Corner Pharmacy at the top of the High Street. Miss Jane Iles was the Principal from about 1850, and the school moved later to Mount Pleasant House, which contin-

ued to be a girls' and boys' private school in turn until the turn of the century.

13 The Dorcas Society was formed for ladies to meet and make clothes for the poor. It is widely associated with the Victorian age, but is clearly defined in the scriptures.

   Acts IX gives us: '... a certain disciple named Tabitha, which by interpretation is called Dorcas: this woman was full of good works and alms deeds which she did .... and all the widows stood by him weeping, and shewing the coats and garments which Dorcas made, while she was with him.'

14 The Rev. David Wassell was a Baptist minister from Bath. He was obviously an old friend of the Thomas family as he was one of the executors of William Thomas's Will (Sarah's father), which accounts for his close association with Charles (who was the co-executor) in dealing with the financial affairs. The Rev. David Wassell appears on the marriage certificate as officiating at Sarah's wedding.

15 William and John were brothers to Sarah and Kate. William Newitt was born in 1821 and John Anderson was born in 1824. They were both in Australia in June 1859 according to notes on the probate of their father's Will. He left them all lands and houses at Fairford, except for the bequests to his daughters, Sarah and Kate. Cottages and the chapel at Meysey Hampton were also left to the two sons jointly 'desiring that they be vested in Trustees for the use of the Baptist Church meeting in that place in perpetuity'. The affairs were obviously administered on their behalf by Sarah and Charles – and later her husband.

16 The Keyworths lived in Fairford in the 1840s. H.G. Keyworth is listed as being a stationer, printer and bookbinder, renting his shop and 'paper hanging warehouse' from Mr Thomas at £14 a year. This was most probably the large shop and workshops which later became Caldicotts in Milton Street – therefore neighbouring the Thomas's house. Mr Keyworth also borrowed cash from his landlord and this got in arrears, together with overdue rent, and both were deducted from the Thomas's account for books, stationery and binding in 1847. From Sarah's numerous references to the Keyworths, visiting them frequently in Cirencester to where they moved, and to their visits to Fairford, the families became and remained very close. Sarah mentions 'the paper room' at Keyworths so it would seem that they continued in that line of business. Sarah also left £20 in her Will to her 'friend Ellen Keyworth'.

17. C. Thurston appears as Broker on recapitulation of shares 'bought for William Thomas, Esq, February 1858'.

18 Kidd remains a bit of a mysterious association. He appears in the front of Sarah's diary for 1865 as living at Blue Hall, Ingleton, Yorkshire.

19 Elizabeth was most likely Richard Page's sister who had appeared on the census of 1851 as servant in the Thomas household. She was three years older than Richard and is listed as a member of the Meysey Hampton chapel.

20 The Ebenezer Chapel was built for the Particular Baptists who withdrew from the Crofts Chapel in 1860. Enlarged to hold seating for a hundred by 1889, the chapel in Coronation Street closed during the First World War. It was converted into a doctors' surgery in the early 1950s and remained so for about thirty years. It is now a private house.

21 The Baptist Chapel in Coxwell Street was rebuilt in 1857. Coxwell Street is one of Cirencester's most complete areas unchanged over the last three hundred years.

22 Frank, often referred to as Francis, and Anna were two of Frise's children who lived close by the chapel.

23 Mrs Joyce was wife of J.G. Joyce who published what remained for a century the definitive book on The Fairford Windows. The massive volume is a careful study and illustration of each of the twenty-eight medieval stained glass windows of St Mary's Church which are world-famous for being the only extant complete set of that date. The book was published in 1872 and, in view of the immense detail and research that went into it, was probably being worked on by the author at the time Sarah was writing.

24 The Rev. William Knibb was a Baptist Missionary in Jamaica. By a strange coincidence, whilst working on this book, I saw the first item to be shown on the BBC television programme *Antiques Roadshow* in Jamaica was a silver inkstand inscribed to the Rev. William Knibb who was a great emancipator of the slaves. His eldest daughter, Catherine, married Captain Thomas Milbourne in 1848 and went with her husband to England and Africa, but on account of impaired health soon returned to Jamaica, where she died at Swarton, near Kittering on 11 October 1858.

The East family referred to as living in Jamaica also in that period, were obviously old friends of the Thomas's and probably went to the West Indies at the same time as the Knibbs's. In the 1851 census, Alice East is shown as a visitor at the Thomas's. She was then aged twelve and described as a scholar, so probably stayed with the family at Fairford for an English schooling. She was born at Leamington Spa in Warwickshire.

25 The custom of drawing lots to determine one's intended love dates back to Roman times. Pepys also writes of drawing lots to find out who was to be his wife's Valentine.

26 According to the Church Book of the Baptized Church of Christ Meysey Hampton, dated December 1862, a British School was opened in connection 'with the afore-mentioned place of worship'.

It is interesting how entrenched in religious politics the development of our educational system was at that time. Not wishing to get embroiled in the vagaries of specific religious authorities, the government of the day granted £20,000 in 1833 to aid private subscription for the building of schools for the education of the 'poorer classes'. This was divided equally between the two denominational societies who had defined their policies for some two decades.

Founded in 1811 was The National Society for the Education of the Poor in the Principles of the Established Church, and, as implied by its lengthy title, originated strictly for Anglican children. Three years later and two words longer The British System for the Education of the Labouring and Manufacturing Classes of Society of Every Religious Persuasion came into being. The impossibly long names became know simply as National and British Schools. It is interesting therefore that in such a small village as Meysey Hampton, already with a thirteenth century church, a British school was established in connection with the Non-Conformists in 1847, while the Church of England children had to wait for the monumental Education Act of 1870 to enforce a school to be built in 1872 as inter-denominational.

27 Alice and Ellen East (see Note 24).

28 Spurgeon was a great preacher of his day. In Farmor's School Log Book there is reference to the school being closed for 'half-holiday to enable the pupils to hear Spurgeon speak'.

29 Fairford was holding a market and fair back in the thirteenth century. Robert, Earl of Gloucester, Lord of Fairford Manor, who levied tolls and stallage for fairs and markets granted by the King, held the main fair on 25 July as the Feast of St James. According to Fairford manorial deeds, fairs were held on 3 May, 28 July and 1 November when Andrew Barker renewed them after obtaining a charter from Charles II. The July fair had lapsed by 1755 and the twice-yearly fairs were set for 14 May and 12 November. The last May fair was held in 1908.

30 Deliberations for a railway line to Fairford were protracted and political, as opposition against the scheme to link Cheltenham to Andoversford thence down the Coln Valley to Fairford, Lechlade and Faringdon waged between the railway company and the numerous landowners. This was the route for which there were meetings in 1861 at both The Bull and Crofts Hall inviting shareholders and subscribers to forward the scheme by the East Gloucestershire Railway to link the GWR main line. Mr Daniel Iles put his name down for £500, a considerable sum in those days, and an indication of how the tradesmen viewed the potential benefit to the town's economy. That scheme never materialised, neither did the plan to link Fairford to Cirencester by rail. Eventually, the East Gloucestershire Railway opened a branch line from Witney to Fairford in 1873. This coincided with the first corn market held in connection with the monthly cattle market. The twenty-one mile single track journey from Oxford to Fairford was punctuated by stops at ten stations. It closed in 1962.

31 Carey and Thomas (Sarah's grandfather) worked together as Baptist missionaries in India, both got into debt and had to take jobs in indigo factories at one time while they were translating and teaching. In 1800 Carey and Thomas bought premises in Serampore which provided them with a home, and room for a boarding school and a printing press. It was here that they produced sections of the Bible printed in Bengali and other Hindu languages.

32 Cirencester Park has been enjoyed by generations of local people for outings and the Woodhouse was one of the buildings, along with the numerous

follies of rusticated stonework which they were able to make use of to shelter or picnic. Pope's Seat is sited at a strategic junction in the woods at the first *rond-point* where Seven Rides meet. It commemorates the collaboration with Alexander Pope, the poet friend of Lord Bathurst, in landscaping the park. Pope wrote: 'I am with Lord Bathurst at my bower ... draw plans for houses and gardens, open avenues, cut glades, plant firs, contrive waterworks, all very fine and beautiful in our own imagination.'

33 Cirencester Mop originated as a statutory hiring fair where agricultural and domestic labour could be 'hired' for a year on the contract of a shilling. Shepherds wore a lock of fleece on their smock, cowmen a whipcord round their hat to betoken their calling. There were Mops for three weeks in succession, the last was called the Runaway Mop when the contract could be rescinded, otherwise it held for a year. Only the fairground element of the old Mops remain today, but they are still an important part of the country calendar.

34 Fairford Market can be traced back to the time of Henry I when the king granted his falconer a charter to hold a market on Tuesdays and Fridays. By the seventeenth century the market was held weekly on Thursdays, and by the nineteenth century it was a monthly affair and had obviously lapsed at the time Sarah was writing. Traditionally confined to a livestock market, corn and cheese were also sold in 1873 when the railway was opened. The success of the new transport was measured by the following May market when 1,500 head of prime fat and store sheep alone were sold. An annual market dinner was held at The Bull for the farmers and tradesmen; the drovers settled for Bangham Barrett's hot pickled onions and strong beer at The Plough – and the magistrates court was kept busy!

35 Enquirers' Meetings were held periodically to bring up cases of the members whose conduct, or absence from services, caused concern. Discipline was meted out accordingly. One of the greatest 'sins' according to the recorded entries was that of having been confirmed or christened in the Parish Church, this, it was decided, was in direct opposition to the principles of Non-Conformity. Other cases included:
a member addicted to frequent public houses oftener than necessary – two members were appointed to visit and admonish him:
'a scandalous report of Brother Kent', but on investigation found to be reported 'at first divulged to the World by Widow Tackley, to the dishonour of religion from a bad motive'. She was suspended until she made confession of her fault;
Jane Trotman was 'investigated' and found 'guilty of gross immorality and therefore excluded';
George Lawrence 'never retrieved his character' – suspended;
William Risby 'guilty of disguising himself by liqueur, so excluded as a disorderly member'.

36 Stidell and Mason were passengers on *Trent*, a British ship, and were taken off by Capt Wilkes on a Northener Man o' War. It was later learned that Stidell and Mason were Southern agents in the American Civil War.

37 Charles died in 1892. His last Will, drawn up in 1889, reveals that he left all his estate to his 'half-sister' Sarah Mary Anne Milbourne for her sole use. Charles Kingsley Milbourne (Sarah's son) was his executor.

38 A Bump Supper was traditionally an all male celebratory supper.

39 Samuel Vines was a maltster who lived at The Green, Fairford. He was also something of a diarist, recording his first visit 'to see the sea' – at the age of forty-two. Such was his father's fear of Napoleon invading England that he had a secret passage built into his house and a form of observation tower on the roof. Samuel would have been in his mid-sixties at the time of Sarah's writing the diary.

40 The magistrates court still stands in the High Street, but unused now for about twenty years.

41 The Belgian sculptor was P. M. van Gelder. He also executed two chimney pieces for Northwick Park, and a fireplace for a small drawing room for Badminton House.

42 Sezincote was built on the fortunes of Sir Charles Cockerall, amassed during his service in the East India Company. The Indian influence in the design of the house and grounds is outstanding both in its architectural composition and incongruity in the heart of Cotswold stone vernacular.

43 The Magpies – an old wayside inn, properly called the Three Magpies – between Fairford and Meysey Hampton. It has been closed for many years and is now a private house.

44 The extraordinary life of John Thomas (Sarah's grandfather) is included in the book *Good and Great Men of Gloucestershire* published by J. Stratford in 1867.

John Thomas was born at Fairford in 1757 and was admitted in 1766 to Farmor's School (established next to the Church in 1738 as Fairford Free School for Boys). His father was deacon of the Baptist Chapel in Milton Street, but John was a vastly different character from his father and his elder brother James, who was remarkable for his piety. John was described as 'a hopeless child', even by his own admission. He truanted from school and rebelled against discipline. He eventually ran away to London and by chance received a training in medicine and surgery at Westminster Hospital. He married Catherine Pratt (after whom Kate was named) and became ship's surgeon on the *Earl of Oxford*, much to the distress of his poor wife who was left penniless following his imprisonment for debt. After a tumultuous and colourful period alternating between perils at sea and serious illness and hasty atoning for his life, he spent time in prison, prayer and mental asylum. Impulsive and eccentric he was said to have 'sorrows bordering on the tragical and joys on the ecstatic'. His conversion to leading a pious life resulted in his achieving the distinction of being the first Baptist Missionary to Bengal.

He had two sons, John and James, both of whom died in infancy. His daughter, Elizabeth Ann, known as Betsy, lived with her mother in India with friends after John Thomas's death in 1801. Following her mother's death two years later, Betsy came to England and stayed with her father's family in Fairford. She was then sixteen years old. She later married Charles Taylor Kingsley of Boughton in the Parish of St John, Worcestershire and had one son, Charles Kingsley. After her first husband's death, Betsy married William Thomas, Baptist Minister of Meysey Hampton and owner of much property in Fairford and Lechlade. He is described on official certificates as Gentleman. Sarah (the diarist) and her sister Kate were children of this second marriage. There were three other children: William and John, who emigrated to Australia, and a daughter, Elizabeth Ann, who was born between the two boys but did not survive infancy.

he had letter from home this morn hastening him back & they
go to Leith tomorrow. he's most sadly disappointed.

Tues. 24th

Kate has had better night, is better to day, came down at 11
I went to Kirn with our friends. I was so curt & queer with
J. that it quite vexed me. says she won't promise now to
marry him & many other queer & haughty things, poor girl I
can't but pity her, for she's much to learn. I was sadly annoyed
at J. kissing her when he s'd good bye. Dr. Boelcher & two
friends who went by train came into the station & recognised me
I walked with him to the market place & he invited me to
go & see them. I had early cups of tea & they all reach'd home at
8. heard of Mr. Brasington's death & Mr. Millers & John Pierce
Mr. Clissold sen'd slept here last night & says he shall dwarf
Fri & hopes to take the. with him, he supp'd here tonight.

Wed. 25th

I feel much more happy about K. she is better, but last
night as I could home I felt dismay'd & have for some days, I
poured out my whole heart to God in prayer for my heart ached
I found him as I have ever done, my strength & my joy,
my heart was lightened for God help'd me to dear my blinded
tears, not being tears gave way to smiles & content, oh what
an unspeakable privilege is prayer, found K. comfortable

Thurs. 26th

Mr. Cornwall call'd this morn s'd he w'd see Kirn bed to
morrow morn. I went & paid Farries, Fowlers, Wakefields
& dear bills. Mr. Clissold came in to tea & then we had
music & singing which he much enjoyed. I must'nt forget
to note the prayer meeting last night the 1st united meeting
between baptists & independents, chapel full, Mr. Clissold
went & much enjoy'd it. The church people are mortified
that 7 or 8 or 9 prayers every night were sustained this wk
the week mostly different men each night) the week before
last & all of them from the poor despised dissenters. so